Speed Mathematics for Prima
Teach Your Kids Speed Math

By Vali Nasser

Copyright © 2012

Online editions may also be available for this title. For more information email: valinasser@gmail.com

All rights reserved by the author. No part of this publication can be reproduced, stored in a retrieval system, or transmitted in any form or by any means, electronic, mechanical, photocopying, recording or otherwise, without the prior permission of the publisher and/ or author.

ISBN-13: 978-1479127238

ISBN-10: 147912723X

Introduction	4
Chapter 1	6
Addition	6
Chapter 2	10
Subtraction	10
Chapter 3	16
Summary of key points	19
Multiplication of Numbers between 10 and 20	20
Summary of key points	21
Chapter 4	23
Multiplying by 10, 100 and 1000	23
Chapter 5	27
Multiplying by 11	27
Chapter 6	34
General rule for multiplying 2 X 2 digits, using a *Speed Method*	34
Chapter 7	38
Base 100	38
Chapter 8	41
Squaring Numbers between 11 & 19 with ease	41
Chapter 9	43
Special case (1)	43
Special case (2)	44
Chapter 10	46
Division	46
Chapter 11	51
Fractions, decimal and percentage equivalents	51
Chapter 12	56
Number Sequences	56
Chapter 13	61

Estimating 61

Estimating is a very important skill and the sooner children can learn it the better. Starting at 9 years of age and re-visiting periodically at 10, 11,12 and even in the early teens is a good idea!....................................61

Chapter 14 65

Chapter 15 68

General approach to 3 X 3 multiplication 68

Chapter 16 75

Fractions 75

Adding and subtracting mixed numbers: 78

Multiplying Fractions 79

Division of Fractions 79

Converting a mixed number to a fraction 80

Multiplying a mixed numbers together 81

Dividing mixed numbers together 82

Chapter 17 84

Proportions and ratios 84

Chapter 18 86

Square Roots and Cube Roots: 86

Chapter 19 90

Introduction to Algebra 90

Chapter 20 96

Algebraic Substitution. 96

Chapter 21 98

Simple Equations 98

Introduction

Speed Mathematics for Primary School teachers (and parents) will help inculcate a high level of Numeracy in their children using both conventional and novel methods. This book is based on two simple premises. The first one, which is well established, is to have high expectations for your children and the second premise is that showing pupils a variety of methods adds more to flexibility and problem solving skills. In addition, research has shown that an increase in numerical proficiency is associated with higher incomes later on in life. This book will not deal with complex techniques or methods that are totally incomprehensible.

This book will start from the basics of addition, subtraction and multiplication and gradually progress to higher levels of number work and even a bit of algebra. This book is suitable for KS2 (in the UK) that is for age groups 7-11 years internationally, although, some topics in this book will also be suitable for older children and some adults too! By the time kids are ten or eleven years old, using methods in this book they will be able to work out 214 - 98, 15 X 9, 27 X 23, 35 X 35, 53 X 11 in their heads, sometimes faster than a calculator. Parents and teachers will of course need to help them by becoming familiar with the techniques themselves first! Paper and pencil will still be required for most questions, but often the answers can be worked out in one line! The pupil's numerical aptitude should increase, particularly if it is relatively low to start with.

Educational researchers have traditionally quite rightly stated that conceptual understanding in mathematics is important. Although this is a correct premise it is not very useful if a student understands what multiplication is but cannot perform the operation in even simple cases! An example will illustrate this point more clearly. It is important that students grasp the idea that 9 X 7 means we have 9 groups occurring 7 times and that if we add up these groups the appropriate number of times we will have the answer. However, if subsequently they cannot work out 9 X 7 then there is a real problem. The premise in this book is that both conceptual understanding and the use of techniques are important. The latter gives the pupil the tools with which to work out the sums.

The smart techniques presented in this book should make number work significantly easier and consequently more rewarding. This will help build confidence that should extend to other areas of mathematics. In this age of ubiquitous use of calculators and computers the use of these techniques is even more important. Experience shows that pupils have lost the ability to estimate. Students often press the wrong keys and they will accept any absurd answer the calculator produces. To be fair schools have and are recognizing this. Sessions exist for the sole use of calculators whereas in other sessions no calculators are allowed. I believe this is the right balanced approach.

Some of the techniques in this book are very different from those taught traditionally and do take time to assimilate. But you will not need endless time to master these; a few minutes of solid work regularly will put your child and perhaps yourself in a different league in a relatively short time. If you are already very numerate or a mathematics teacher, some of the material will already be familiar to you.

The primary purpose of this book is to introduce pupils to **Speed Methods** that will help students perform better in mathematics. This, in turn, will build confidence and increase self-esteem.

The experience of various teachers who have taught this system suggests that children gain enormous confidence in number operations and their new expertise extends to other areas of mathematics. Adults who have found numerical work difficult in the past will also find the techniques immediately useful in working out every day problems such as percentages and in estimating calculations. Algebra will become less perplexing. The speed methods given in this book are not a panacea. However, its intrinsically rewarding properties facilitate learning. Number work and Algebra are the building blocks of mathematics. This book, I believe, will be a valuable addition to the primary school mathematics curriculum.

As stated before, although the material in this book is primarily aimed at ages 7 to 11, many older students will find it useful as well.

Chapter 1

Addition

The Number Line

When kids progress in their ability to do addition after using counters and fingers, they are often taught the number line method to facilitate their adding skills further. This is certainly a useful method at an early stage. For 7 year olds and older it can be a good reminder. Also remind them that addition can be done in any order. So when working out 7 + 2, we will get the same answer as 2 + 7. This is called the commutative law in mathematics.

Using the Number line method:

Example 1:

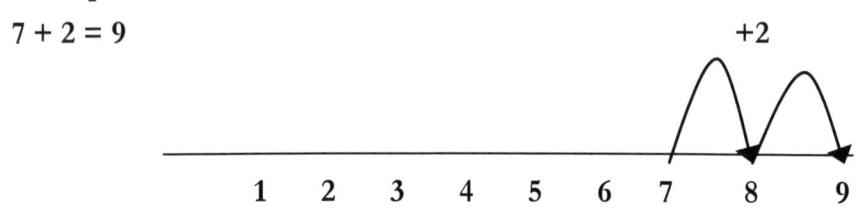

7 + 2 = 9

Example 2

18 + 5 = 23

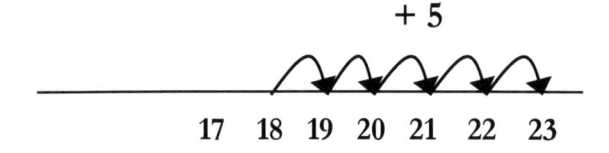

Starting from 18 as shown above, we add 5 to get to 23 on the number line

Breaking down or Partitioning method

As kids become more familiar with double digit additions using the number line method it is worth looking at some faster methods. The break down method is simply a method where you first break down the double digit numbers into tens and units and then add appropriately as shown. With practice children can become quite proficient and move on to 3 digit figures which include the hundreds column as shown in example 3

Ex1

27 + 24

= 27 + 20 + 4 (break down 24 into 20 and 4)

= 47 + 4

= 51

Ex2

42 + 57

= 42 + 50 + 7 (break down 57 into 50 and 7)

= 92 + 7

= 99

Ex 3

122 + 177

= 122 + 170 + 7 (breakdown 177 into 170 and 7)

= 292 + 7

= 299

Column Addition Method

This is the most popular method taught for older primary school children, starting at 7 or 8 years old and re-visiting periodically. In this method, children learn to add the unit columns first and carry the digits to the tens, likewise add the tens and carry appropriately to the hundreds and so on. Two examples are shown below:

```
      47              249
    + 38            + 572
      85              821
       1              1 1
```

Column addition is a good traditional method when used with larger whole numbers and decimals – however for some situations a special speed method can be very helpful

This *Speed Method* below will help kids in mental arithmetic. Nine year olds and of course older children too, may find it useful.

Compensating or adjusting method

In this method we simply adjust by adding or subtracting from the rounded up or rounded down number as shown in the examples below.

Ex1

96 + 69 =

100 – 4 + 70 – 1 =

170 – 5 = 165

Ex2

59 + 88 +23 =

60 – 1 + 90 – 2 + 20 + 3 =:

150 + 20 – 3 + 3 =

170

Now try these using any method prefered

Ex1A

(1) 7 + 18 =

(2) 12 +19 =

(3) 16 +28 =

(4) 56 +129 =

(5) 68 +38 =

(6) 78 +98 +29 =

(7) 128 +239 +18 =

(8) 127 +452 + 389 =

Summary:

As kids become familiar with different methods of addition, they will have different strategies to fall back on. This in fact will increase their mental flexibility and gradually enable them to perform faster calculations. Remind them that when adding the order in which they do it does not matter. In mathematics this is known as the commutative law.

That is, $a + b = b + a$

It is important to point out that the order of addition does not make any difference – no need to confuse them with the word 'commutative' at this stage.

Example: $13 + 8 = 21$ and so does $8 + 13 = 21$

This is also true for multiplication, for example 5×4 is the same as 4×5 both the answers $= 20$

However, it is important to illustrate that the commutative law does not apply for subtraction or division.

E.g. $15 - 7$ is obviously not the same as $7 - 15$

Similarly $3 \div 4$ is not the same as $4 \div 3$

Chapter 2

Subtraction

This chapter will be useful for children who are 7 - 11 years old. Hopefully, children will have done some basic subtractions using single digit numbers by the age of 6 and 7 years. Using counters and taking away or using fingers and folding them up are some of the ways taught at a very early age.

Now, consider the number line method which will prove useful as an additional tool.

Example1:

Work out 67 - 39

Working backwards, start from 39 and count till 67 using the number line if necessary as shown:

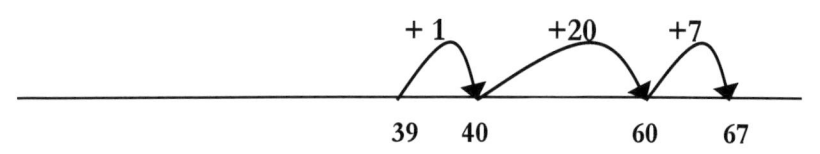

```
         +1        +20       +7
        ╱╲       ╱────╲     ╱╲
────────────────────────────────────
        39  40           60    67
```

Since 1 + 20 + 7 = 28, so 67 - 39 = 28

(The difference from 39 to 40 is 1, then from 40 to 60 the difference is 20 and finally the difference from 60 to 67 is 7, so adding up 1 + 20 + 7 = 28 as shown)

Example 2:

(No need for number lines once they get familiar with the principle)

Work out 117 – 48

So working backwards from 48 we can reason as follows::

The difference between 48 and 50 is 2, then from 50 to 100 the difference is 50 and finally from 100 to 117 the difference is 17. Now as before add up 2 +50 +17 to give 69 as the answer.

Before we look at one more speed method let us re-visit the traditional column subtraction method.

Traditional column method

The traditional methods of subtraction serve us well in mathematics.

However, there is one more strategy that we can use to make this process much easier but more of this later. First we will consider the normal approach.

Consider the following example:

$$241$$
$$-\ \ 28$$
$$\overline{}$$
$$213$$

Starting from the right hand side we cannot subtract 8 from 1 so we borrow 1 from the tens column to make the units column 11. Subtracting 8 from 11 gives us 3. However since we have taken away 1 from the tens column we are left with 3 in this column. Subtracting 2 from 3 in the tens column gives us 1. Since we have nothing else to take away the final answer is 213.

Now consider the same problem using a smart strategy.

If we add 2 to the top and bottom number we get:

$$243 \quad (241+2)$$
$$-\ \ 30 \quad (28+2)$$
$$\overline{}$$
$$213$$

You can see that subtracting 30 from 243 is easier than subtracting 28 from 241!

This strategy relies on the algebraic fact that if you add or subtract the same number to the top and bottom numbers you do not change the answer of the subtraction sum.

Algebra for those teachers or parents interested: consider the problem a-b

If we add any number n to both a and b and then do the subtraction we obtain:

$(a + n) - (b + n) = a + n - b - n = a - b$ as before.

The same is true if you subtract n from both sides.

$(a - n) - (b - n) = a - n - b + n = a - b$

So essentially we try and add or subtract a certain number to both the numbers in order to make the sum simpler. A few more examples will help.

Example 1:
$$113$$
$$- 6$$

Add 4 to both numbers (we want to try to make the units column 0 in the bottom row if we can and if it helps)

So the new sum is:
$$117$$
$$- 10$$
$$107$$

We can see that if we subtract 10 from 117 we get 107.

Example 2:
$$321$$
$$- 114$$

Let us add 6 to each number so that the unit column in the bottom number becomes a 0 as shown below:

$$327 \text{ (add 6 to 321)}$$
$$- 120 \text{ (add 6 to 114)}$$
$$207$$

Subtracting 120 from 327 we get 207 as shown. No borrowing is required.

Example 3:
$$623$$
$$- 158$$

Add 2 to both numbers so we get:

```
    625     (add 2 to 623)
  - 160     (add 2 to 158)
  _____
```

Now, we can add 40 to each number as this makes the tens column 0 as shown.

```
    665     (add 40 to 625)
  - 200     (similarly, add 40 to 160)
  _____
    465
```

This subtraction is obviously much easier. Sometimes it is easier to revert to the traditional method. But if students find borrowing from the preceding column difficult then this strategy can be very useful.

Now try these using the number line or any method you like to work out the following:

Ex2A: (useful for 7- 8 year olds)

(1) 10 – 7

(2) 12 - 8

(3) 20 - 7

(4) 15 – 6

(5) 22 -18

(6) 25 -17

(7) 33 -18

(8) 45 -28

(9) 42 -17

(10) 30 -11

Ex 2B (useful for 8 - 11 year olds and older pupils as required)

These are slightly harder so you might want to try the number line or the adjusting method to work these out:

(1) 212 – 18

(2) 213 – 17

(3) 2124 -118

(4) 321 – 118

(5) 615 –156

(6) 532 – 127

(7) 897 – 269

(8) 1009 - 878

Now consider a fast method for subtracting from 100, 1000 or 10000

In this case we use the rule **'all from nine and the last from 10'**

Example 1: 100 -76

We simply take each figure (except the last) in 76 from 9 and the last from 10 as shown below:

```
  1 0 0
-    76
     24
```

Take 7 from 9 to give 2 and take 6 from 10 to give 4

Example 1: 1000 – 897 =103

We simply take each figure (except the last) in 897 from 9 and the last from 10 as shown below:

```
 1 0 0 0
 - 8 9 7
   1 0 3
```

(Take 8 from 9 to give 1. Take 9 from 9 to give 0 and take 7 from 10 to give 3)

Example 2: 10,000 – 8743

$$\begin{array}{r}10000\\-8743\\\hline 1257\end{array}$$

(Take 8 from 9 to give 1, 7 from 9 to give 2, 4 from 9 to give 5 and finally 7 from 10 to give 3)

Now try these.

Ex2C:

(1) 1000– 657

(2) 100 – 67

(3) 1000 –507

(4) 10000 – 8989

(5) 10000 – 9998

(6) 100 – 64

(7) 10000 – 9898

(8) 10000 –786

(9) 1000 – 21

Chapter 3

Multiplication

Primary school teachers and parents try their best to get kids to learn their tables. There are many methods including, of course, the 'famous' rote method. Sadly, despite best efforts, many children fail to learn their tables beyond the 4X or 5X tables. Firstly, remind them that the order in which they do multiplication does not matter (the commutative law applies) – that is 3 X 4 is the same as 4 X 3. However do not despair if at this stage they only know their two and three times tables. Progress can still be made using 'speed methods'. For example, if they know how to double numbers, they can learn to multiply by 4. Since 4 X 6 is simply 2 X (2 X 6) = 2 X 12 =24. Doubling numbers is a very important skill. An easy way to double larger numbers is as follows: To work out 2 X 37, you can break it up as 2 X 30 + 2 X 7 = 60 + 14 =74. Let's look at another example: work out 2 X 46. In this case re-write 2 X 46 as 2 X 40 + 2 X 6 = 80 +12 =92 or if you want to start kids with simpler examples try working out 2 X 14 = 2 X 10 + 2 X 4 =20 + 8 =28.

In addition if children know their 3 X tables, perhaps at a stretch they can do their 6X tables. For example 6 X 5 = 2 X (3 X 5) = 2 X 15 =30 Hopefully, by the age of 7 or 8 years, they should know at least their 1X, 2X, 3X, 4X and possibly 5X tables Remind them that 0 X any number =0. So that 5 X 0= 0, 11 X 0 =0 and so on.

The difficulty is often encountered in learning 7 X, 8 X, 9 X and 12X tables. We will look at a spectacular *'Speed Method'* way for working out multiplications near base 10. This method is from a system called 'Vedic Mathematics' which in this case uses base 10 as a reference point for single digit multiplications. By the time children are 9 years old they should know their times tables to 12X. This chapter will thus be useful to children in the UK in KS2 or in terms of age for those between 7 and 11 years of age.

Let us look at a '*Speed Method* 'to multiply numbers near 10.

Example 1: Multiply 7 X 8

Step 1:

Re-write the sum vertically and work out the deficiency between 10 and each of the numbers on the left hand column. Place the results in the right hand column as shown.

Original Numbers	Deficiency from 10
7	−3
8	−2

Step 2:

(Notice the minus sign on the right hand side, which shows how much less is each number on the left from 10)

The answer is in two parts. See arrows below. The first part is found by subtracting the two numbers across the arrows shown. That is, either 7 – 2=5 OR, 8 – 3=5. It does not matter which diagonal you use to do the cross subtraction. The second part is found by multiplying the two numbers in the second vertical column, 3 X 2=6.

So the answer is 56.

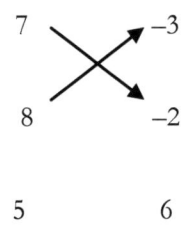

```
    7           –3
      ╲       ╱
        ╳
      ╱       ╲
    8           –2

    5            6
```

(For those interested, note that the left hand number corresponds to the base number, so 5 means 5 tens)

Example 2: Work out 6 X 9

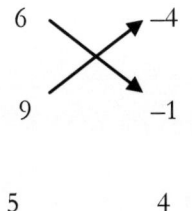

```
    6           –4
      ╲       ╱
        ╳
      ╱       ╲
    9           –1

    5            4
```

As stated previously, write down the numbers to be multiplied vertically on the left hand side. So 6 X 9 is written 6 and 9. On the right hand side we write down the deficiency between 10 and each number. The answer is in two parts. The first part is found by subtracting any two numbers diagonally as shown by the arrows. E.g. 9 – 4=5 OR 6 – 1=5 (It does not matter which two numbers diagonally you take). The second part is simply the multiple of the two numbers (4 & 1) on the vertical right hand side. 4 X 1=4

So the answer is 54.

We will now go through an example where a carry over is required.

Example 3: Work out 6 X 7

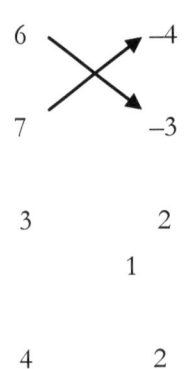

```
    6           -4
      ╲       ╱
        ╳
      ╱       ╲
    7           -3


    3           2
            1


    4           2
```

The answer is in two parts. The first part is found by subtracting any two numbers across the arrows shown. This gives you 3. The second part is simply the multiple of the two numbers (4 & 3) on the vertical right hand side (4 X 3=12). In this case we put down 2 and carry over the 1 as shown so the final answer is 42. (Since 3+1 carried over =4)

We will do one more question with carry over to consolidate this method.

Example 4: Let us try and multiply 6 X 5 using this method

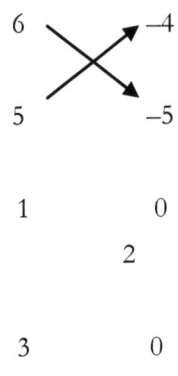

```
    6           -4
      ╲       ╱
        ╳
      ╱       ╲
    5           -5


    1           0
            2


    3           0
```

The answer is in two parts. The first part is found by subtracting any two numbers across the arrows shown. This gives you 1. The second part is simply the multiple of the two numbers (4 & 5) on the vertical right hand side. 4 X 5=20. In this case we put down 0 and carry over the 2 as shown. The final answer is 30. (Since 1+2 carried over =3)

Now try these :

Ex3A:

    (1) 7 X 8

    (2) 8 X 9

    (3) 9 X 7

    (4) 8 X 8

    (5) 7 X 9

    (6) 9 X 9

    (7) 5 X 7

    (8) 5 X 8

Summary of key points

The key rule here is to work vertically and crosswise using base 10.

(1) Set the sum up vertically and work out the deficiencies from 10

(2) The answer is in two parts

(3) The first part is the difference diagonally across

(4) The last part is found by multiplying the two numbers vertically on the right hand side

(5) Remember to carry over if necessary to the left hand side

Why does base10 arithmetic work?

Consider the algebraic expression $(10-a)(10-b)$, where a and b are single digit numbers to be multiplied.

Expanding the bracket we have:

$(10 - a)(10 - b) = 100 - 10a - 10b + ab$

So $ab = (10 - a)(10 - b) + 10a + 10b - 100$

So $ab = 10(a + b - 10) + (10 - a)(10 - b)$

If a=7 and b =8

Then 7 X 8 = 10(7+8 −10)+3 X 2

             =10 X 5 +6

             =56

which is the correct answer

Multiplication of Numbers between 10 and 20

Multiplication of 2-digit numbers near base 10, and the numbers being multiplied are above 10.

Example 1: 12 X 13

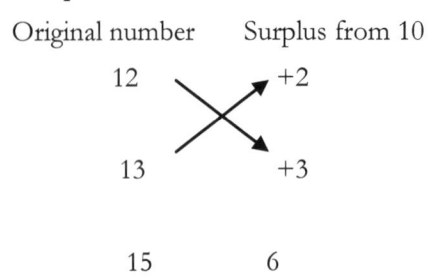

Original number   Surplus from 10

```
    12            +2
       ╲       ╱
        ╲   ╱
         ╳
        ╱   ╲
       ╱       ╲
    13            +3


    15             6
```

(We put a plus sign on the right hand side to denote that the number 12 is 2 more than 10, hence +2)

This is similar to the method we have already used. The only difference to note is that in the right hand vertical column the numbers have a + sign in front of them. This is to remind you that when you do your crosswise sum you add the diagonal numbers instead of subtracting. Again you may use any diagonal to do this addition.

Step 1: 12 is 2 more than 10, so the right hand number is +2

Similarly, 13 is 3 more than 10, so the right hand number is +3

Step 2: Cross add diagonally to get 15 and multiply the two digits vertically on the right (2 X 3) to get 6

Step 3: the answer is the first part and the second part written together, which in this case is 156

Another two examples will help consolidate this method.

Example 2: Work out 14 X 12

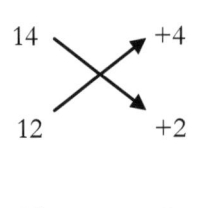

```
    14            +4
       ╲       ╱
        ╲   ╱
         ╳
        ╱   ╲
       ╱       ╲
    12            +2


    16             8
```

Using the crosswise and vertical rule you will see that the first part is 16 (14+2 or 12+4)

and the second part is 4 X 2=8. So the answer to 14 X 12 is 168

Now we will do a final example involving a carry over.

Example 3: Work out 15 X 13

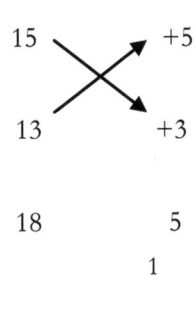

```
    15          +5
       ╲     ╱
         ╳
       ╱     ╲
    13          +3

    18          5
            1
```

Answer = 195

Step 1: +5, is 5 more than 10. Similarly, +3 is 3 more than 10

The crosswise sum is 18. (15+3=18 or 13+5=18)

Step 2: Multiplying vertically the numbers on the right we have 15 (3 X 5), so we need to carry 1 as shown.

Step 3: The answer is 195 (since 8+1 =9)

Summary of key points

The key rule here is to work vertically and crosswise using base 10.

(1) Set the sum up vertically and work out the surpluses from 10

(2) The answer is in two parts

(3) The first part is found by adding diagonally across

(4) The last part is found by multiplying the two numbers vertically on the right hand side

(5) Remember to carry over if necessary to the left hand side

What about multiplying numbers with decimals?

This will be useful for 10 and 11 year olds, especially those aiming for grammar schools in the UK or equivalent internationally.

Example 1: Multiply 12X1.3

Use the method above to work out 12X13. We know the answer is 156. Note the fact that 1.3 is 13 divided by 10. So the answer is simply 156 divided by 10 =15.6. **We will look at decimal multiplication in more detail later.**

Now try these:

Ex3B

(1) 13 X 14
(2) 15 X 13
(3) 16 X 12
(4) 13 X 12
(5) 15 X 14
(6) 16 X 17
(7) 15 X 18

Chapter 4

Multiplying by 10, 100 and 1000

Most children by the time they are 8 or 9 years old can multiply by 10 but some become stuck when multiplying by 100 or 1000.

This chapter will thus be useful in extending this knowledge for 8 -11 year olds. Before we look at speed methods we will look at the traditional method first.

Traditional method

The traditional method of multiplying by a 10, 100, 1000 is shown below. This method is useful as it cements the conceptual understanding required. However, when pupils cannot multiply 234 X 100 straight away we need to resort to another simple technique to help them. We will explore this obvious technique later. Firstly, let us review the traditional technique.

Consider having to work out 34 X 10

This chapter also explains **place value**. For example for the number 34, the right hand digit is the units digit and the number 3 on the left hand side is the tens digit or column. In fact every time you move one place to the left you increase the value by 10. So moving left by one place from the tens column we get the 100's column as shown below.

Hundreds	Tens	Units
	3	4

When we multiply by 10 each digit moves one column to the left. So 34 X 10 =340 as shown below. In other words 3 tens becomes 3 hundreds, the 4 units becomes 4 tens as shown. Also notice we have 0 units so we must put a zero in the units column. Moving each digit 1 place to the left has the effect of making it 10 X bigger.

Hundreds	Tens	Units
3	4	0

Consider the sum 34 X 100

Multiplying by 100 is similar. We simply multiply by 10 and then 10 again. This has the effect of moving each digit two places to the left. This makes it 100 X bigger.

The number 34 is shown below as 3 tens and 4 units.

Thousands	Hundreds	Tens	Units
		3	4

We will now do the multiplication and see its effect.

Clearly multiplying 34 by 100 has the effect of moving the 3 in the tens column to the thousands column and the 4 units to the hundreds column. This is shown below.

Thousands	Hundreds	Tens	Units
3	4	0	0

So 34 X 100 =3400 as shown above.

This technique is important as it illustrates the concept of multiplying by 10 or 100 taking place. The same process applies to multiplying by 1000, 10,000 or a higher power of 10.

Also note, there is a short hand way of writing 100, 1000, 10,000 and larger powers of 10.

$100 = 10^2$ (10 squared, which is 10 X 10)

$1000 = 10^3$ (10 cubed which is 10 X 10 X 10)

$10,000 = 10^4$ ((10 to the power 4, which is 10 X 10 X 10 X 10)

$1000,000 = 10^6$ (10 to the power 6 which is 10 X 10 X 10 X 10 X 10 X 10)

Higher powers can be written similarly.

Dividing by 10, 100 and 1000.

Conceptually, dividing by 10, 100 or 1000 is a similar process, except, on this occasion, you move the digits to the right by the appropriate number of places.

Consider having to divide 34 by 10.

Which, is 3 tens and 4 units becomes 3 units and 4 tenths as shown.

Hundreds	Tens	Units	Tenths
		3	4

The rationale for this is that we move each digit to the right. So 3 tens becomes 3 units and 4 units becomes 4 tenths as shown above. The answer is written as 3.4. Similarly when dividing by 100 or a 1000 the number is moved two and three places to the right as appropriate. We will now look at the technique below to work out the answer mechanically. This ensures you get the right answer without having to resort to the thousands, hundreds, tens, units, tenths and hundredths column. The simple rules shown below may help those students who find the above process difficult.

Speed Method: Rule for multiplying whole numbers:

(1) When multiplying a whole number by 10 add a zero at the end of the number.

(2) When multiplying by 100 add two zeros.

(3) When multiplying by 1000 add three zeros

(4) You simply add the number of zeros reflected in the power of 10.

Some examples will illustrate this:

  (1) 45 X 10 =450 (add 1 zero to 45)

  (2) 67 X 100=6700 (add 2 zeros to 67)

  (3) 65 X 1000=65000 (add 3 zeros to 65)

  (4) 65788 X 1000000 = 65788000000 (add 6 zeros to 65788)

Speed Method: Rules for numbers with decimals:

When multiplying by 10, 100, 1000 move the decimal place the appropriate number of places to the right.

(1) 67.5 X 10 =675 (the decimal point is moved 1 place to the right to give us 675.0 which is the same as 675)

(2) 67.5 X 100 =6750 (this time move the decimal point two places to the right to give 6750.0 which is the same as 6750)

(3) 6.87 X 1000 =6870 (in this case move the decimal point three places to the right to give the required answer.)

Now consider examples involving division by 10, 100 and 1000.

(1) 450 ÷ 10 = 45 (You simply remove one zero from the number)

(2) 45 ÷ 100=0.45 (similarly move the decimal point two places to the left to give us 0.45)

(3) 345.78 ÷ 100 =3.4578 (Again simply move the decimal point 2 places to the left)

(4) 456.78 ÷ 1000 =0.45678 (Move the decimal point 3 places to the left)

Now try these questions using the fast technique.

Ex4A:

(1) 456 X 100

(2) 54.8 X 10

(3) 78.87 X 1000

(4) 678 X 100

(5) 67 ÷ 10

(6) 687 ÷ 100

(7) 765 ÷ 1000

(8) 897 ÷ 100

(9) 87.12 ÷ 100

(10) 67 ÷ 1000

Chapter 5

More Multiplication

In this chapter we will look at some fascinating ways of quickly multiplying by 11, 9, 12 and 5, which will motivate kids further.

Multiplying by 11

In schools many pupils can multiply by 11 and some pupils even use good techniques to speed up their calculations. One common method used is to multiply by 10 and then add the number itself. We will now look at a super-efficient method that is rarely used.

Super-efficient *Speed Method*:

11 X 11 =121 (the first and last numbers are the same & the middle number is the sum of the first two digits)

The basic method is: Start with the first number, add the next two, until the last one. This method works with any number of digits.

Let us explore a few more examples with two digit numbers.

13 X 11= 143 (Keep the first and last digit of the number 13 the same, add 1 & 3 to give the middle number 4)

14 X 11= 154

15 X 11= 165

18 X 11= 198

19 X 11= 1(10)9=209 (Notice the middle number is 10, since 1+9=10, so we need to carry 1 to the left hand number.)

A few more examples will show the power of this method.

27 X 11= 297 (the first number=2, the middle number=2+7, the last number =7)

28 X 11=2(10)8= 308 (using similar analysis to 19 X 11 above)

The same principle applies to numbers with more than 2 digits.

Example 1: Work out 412 X 11

412 X 11 = 4532 (The first number is the first digit of the multiplicand, the second number is the sum of the first two digits, the third number is the sum of the second and third digit, and finally we have the last digit)

Example 2: Work out 13212 X 11

13212 X 11 = 145332 (As before the first number is the first digit of the multiplicand, the second number is the sum of the first two digits, the third number is the sum of the next two digits and so on until the last digit)

Now try these by yourself.

Ex5A

(1) 23 X 11
(2) 41 X 11
(3) 45 X 11
(4) 56 X 11
(5) 34 X 11
(6) 33 X 11

Summary:

To multiply a 2-digit number by 11 the answer has 3 parts:

The first part is the first digit of the number, the last part is the last digit of the number and the middle part is the sum of the first and second digits.

We can use the same technique to multiply 3 or more digit numbers by 11.

> In this case start with the first number, add next two numbers, then the subsequent two digits. Continue this process until the last number

Multiplying quickly by 9.

Here is another easy method to work out the 9X table

Example1: Work out 9X2

Method: Step1: Add '0' to the number you are going to multiply by 9, e.g. 2 to get 20

Step2: Now subtract 2 from 20 to get 18, which is the final answer

Example 2: Work out 9X7

Method: Step1: Add '0' to the number you are going to multiply by 9, e.g. 7 to get 70

Step2: Now subtract 7 from 70 to get 63 which is the final answer

Example 3: Work out 9 X 12

Method: Step1: Add '0' to the number you are going to multiply by 9, e.g. 12 to get 120

Step2: Now subtract 12 from 120 to get 108 which is the final answer

Example 4: Work out 9 X 35

Method: Step1: Add '0' to the number you are going to multiply by 9, e.g. 35 to get 350

Step2: Now subtract 35 from 350 to get 315 which is the final answer

Essential Method: $6 \times 9 = 6(10 - 1) = 60 - 6 = 54$

Try these:

Ex 5B

    (1) 9 X 7

    (2) 9 X 9

(3) 9 X 12

(4) 9 X 14

(5) 9 X 17

(6) 9 X 22

(7) 9 X 21

(8) 9 X 24

Similarly there is neat method to multiply any number by 12

Example1: Work out 8 X 12

Method: Multiply 8 by 10 then add to it double of 8

8 X 10 = 80
Double 8 = 16
80 +16 = 96
Hence 8 X 12 = 96

Example2: Work out 27 X 12

First work out 27 X 10, which equals 270
Now double 27 (or 2X 27) = 54
Hence 27 X 12 = 270 + 54 = 324

Example 3: Work out 75 X 12

75 X 12 = 750 + 2X75
= 750 + 150 = 900
Hence 75 X 12 = 900

Ex 5C

   (1) 6 X 12

   (2) 8 X 12

   (3) 13 X 12

   (4) 16 X 12

   (5) 18 X 12

   (6) 22 X 12

Multiplication by 5

Before you start the 5X table method remind your pupils or your child of even and odd numbers!

Even numbers are all numbers divisible by 2

e.g. 2, 4, 6, 8, 10, 12, 14, 16, 18, 20, 22, 24, 26, 28, 30, 32, 34, 36, 38, 40,

Odd numbers are those numbers not divisible by 2

e.g. 1, 3, 5, 7, 9, 11, 13, 15, 17, 19, 21, 23, 25, 27, 29, 31, 33, 35, 37,

Now look at the 5X table below:

5 X 1 = 5 (1, is odd so the answer ends in 5)

5 X 2 = 10 (2, is even so the answer ends in zero)

5 X 3 =15 (3, is odd so the answer ends in 5)

5 X 4 =20 (4, is even so the answer ends in zero)

5 X 5 =25 (5, is odd so the answer ends in 5)

5 X 6 =30 (6, is even so the answer ends in zero)

5 X 7 = 35 (7, is odd so the answer ends in 5)

5 X 8 = 40 (8, is even so the answer ends in zero)

5 X 9 =45 (9, is odd so the answer ends in 5)

5 X 10 =50 (10, is even so the answer ends in zero)

5 X 11 = 55 (11, is odd so the answer ends in 5)

5 X 12 =60 (12, is even so the answer ends in zero)

5 X 13 =65 (13, is even so the answer ends in 5)

5 X 14 =70 (14, is even so the answer ends in zero)

5 X 15 =75 (15, is even so the answer ends in 5)

5 X 16 =80 (16, is even so the answer ends in zero)

5 X 17 =85 (17, is even so the answer ends in 5)

5 X 18 =90 (18, is even so the answer ends in zero)

5 X19 = 95 (19, is even so the answer ends in 5)

5 X 20 =100 (20, is even so the answer ends in zero)

Notice that all odd numbers multiplied by 5 end in 5!

All even numbers multiplied by 5 end in 0

Look at the even numbers again:

5 X 2 =10

5 X 4 =20

5 X 6 =30

5 X 8 =40

5 X 10 =50

5 X 12 =60

(The pattern for even numbers is 10,20,30,40 50 & 60!)

Now look at the odd numbers:

5 X 1 = 5

5 X 3 = 15

5 X 5 =25

5 X 7 =35

5 X 9 =45

5 X 11 =55

(The pattern for odd numbers is 5, 15, 25, 35, 45 & 55)

Another way of multiplying by 5

Multiply the number by 10 and halve the answer!

Example 1: 5 X 4 = half of 10 X 4 = half of 40 = 20

Example 2: 5 X 6 = half of 10 X 6 = half of 60 =30

Example 3: 5 X 3 = half of 10 X 3 = half of 30 = 15

Ex 5D

(1) 5 X 6 =   (2) 5 X 3 =   (3) 5 X 5 =   (4) 5 X 7 =
(5) 5 X 2 =   (6) 5 X 8 =   (7) 5 X 9 =

Chapter 6

General rule for multiplying 2 X 2 digits, using a *Speed Method*

The method below gives you a general rule that always works.
There is no need to consider bases.

Example1: Work out 22 X 31

$$\begin{array}{r} 22 \\ \times\ 31 \\ \hline \end{array}$$

= First part, middle part, last part

We will work out the middle part last.

The first part is 2 X 3 =6 (Multiply the vertical left hand digits together)

The last part is 2 X 1=2 (Multiply the vertical right hand digits together)

The middle part is 2 X 1+2 X 3 =8 (cross multiply the digits and add)

So the answer is 682 (first part plus=6, middle part =8 and last part =2)

This is also shown with appropriate arrows below:

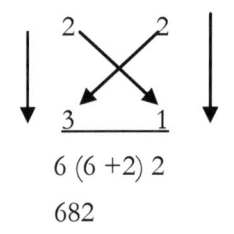

$$\begin{array}{c} 2 \quad\ \ 2 \\ \downarrow \times \downarrow \\ 3 \quad\ \ 1 \\ 6\ (6+2)\ 2 \\ 682 \end{array}$$

The first part is found by multiplying the first two vertical digits as shown by the first arrow. This gives us 6. Likewise, the last part is found by multiplying the last two vertical digits together which gives us 2 as shown. The middle part is found by cross multiplying and adding as shown..

So the middle part is 3 X 2 +2 X 1 = 6 +2 =8

Example 2: Work out 41 X 21

$$\begin{array}{r} 41 \\ \times\ 21 \\ \hline =\quad 861 \end{array}$$

The first part is 4 X 2 =8 (Multiply the vertical left hand digits together)
The last part is 1 X 1=1 (Multiply the vertical right hand digits together)
The middle part is 4 X 1+1 X 2 =6 (cross multiply the digits and add)
So the answer is 861 (first part plus=8, middle part =6 and last part =1)

Example 3: Work out 72 X 21

$$\begin{array}{r} 7\ 2 \\ \text{X}\ \underline{2\ 1} \\ 14\ \ 1\ 2 \\ 1 \\ \\ 1512 \end{array}$$

Here we can see the first part is 14, the last part is 2.

The middle is 7 X 1 + 2 X 2 = 11 so we put down 1 and carry 1. This gives us 1512 as the final answer.

One more example will help us consolidate this important method.

Example 4: Work out 58 X 34

$$\begin{array}{r} 5\ 8 \\ \text{X}\ \underline{3\ 4} \\ 15\ 4\ 2 \\ 4\ 3 \\ \\ 1972 \end{array}$$

The first part is 5 X 3=15. The last part is 8 X 4=32 (put down the 2 and carry the 3). The middle part is 5 X 4+8 X 3 =44 (again put down the 4 and carry the 4). This gives us 1972 as the final answer as shown

Multiplying a two digit number by a single digit number:

Example 5: Work out 58 X 4

We simply re-write as 58 X 04 and multiply as before:

$$\begin{array}{r} 5\ 8 \\ \times\ 0\ \underline{4} \\ 0\ 2\ 0\ 2 \\ 3 \end{array}$$

$$232$$

The first part is 5 X 0=0. The last part is 8 X 4=32 (put down the 2 and carry the 3). The middle part is 5 X 4+8 X 0 =20. This, gives us 232 as the final answer as shown

Example 6: Work out 82 X 8

As before: re-write: 82 X 08

$$\begin{array}{r} 8\ 2 \\ \times\ 0\ \underline{8} \\ 0\ 646 \\ 1 \end{array}$$

$$656$$

The first part is 8 X 0=0. The last part is 2 X 8=16 (put down the 6 and carry the 1). The middle part is 8 X 8+2 X 0 =64. This gives us 656 as the final answer as shown

Summary

We now have several methods to work with:
    (1) Working with base 10 & 20

(2) Multiplying by 11

(3) **General vertical & crosswise multiplication for any 2 digit multiplication**

At first it will seem confusing as to which method to use. However, with practice you will soon see the value of one method over another depending on the multiplication sum.

The Grid Method of Multiplication

This is a very powerful method for children who find traditional long multiplication methods difficult. The grid method is hence a good technique for multiplication that pupils may prefer in many instances.

Consider the example 12 **X** 13

To work this out using the grid method, re-write 12 as 10 and 2, and 13 as 10 and 3 as shown on the outside of the grid table.

X	10	2
10	100	20
3	30	6

Multiply out the outside horizontal numbers with the outside vertical numbers to get the numbers inside as shown. Finally, just add up the inside numbers which in this case is 100+20+30+6 =156

Let us try another example: Multiply 37 X 6

Re-write the number 37 as 30 and 7 and re-write as shown in the grid table.

X	30	7
6	180	42

So the answer is 180+42 =222

Chapter 7

Re-visiting base arithmetic

Base 100

For children in interested in further speedy number crunching these base arithmetic methods may prove useful.

Consider the sum 95 X 88

Using base 100, we can write the sum as below.

Original numbers   Deficiency from 100

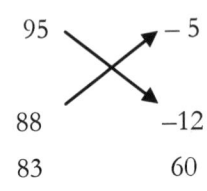

```
    95           − 5
       ╲       ╱
        ╲     ╱
         ╲   ╱
          ╳
         ╱   ╲
        ╱     ╲
    88           −12
    83            60
```

8360

You can see that by using crosswise subtraction and vertical multiplication we get 83 and 60 respectively. 83 is the first part obtained by crosswise subtraction & 60 is the second part obtained by vertical multiplication of the right hand column.

Example 2: Work out 93 X 99

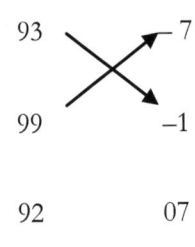

```
    93           − 7
       ╲       ╱
        ╳
       ╱       ╲
    99           −1
    92            07
```

9207

Using crosswise subtraction we get 92. Using right hand column vertical multiplication we get 7. Notice since we are working with base 100, when we get a single digit we have to insert a 0. We can see we have 07 on the right hand side. The answer is then 9207.

Now let us consider numbers just over 100.

Example 3: Work out 103 X 107

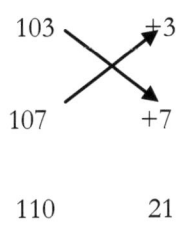

```
103         +3
    ╲    ╱
     ╲  ╱
      ╲╱
      ╱╲
     ╱  ╲
107         +7

110        21
```

11021

Notice this time we have +3 and +7 on the right hand side. This denotes that 103 is 3 more than 100 and 107 is 7 more than 100. Using the crosswise method we get 110. (Since we add the numbers this time, finally using right hand column vertical multiplication we get 21. Hence the answer is 11020.)

Now let us look at an example requiring a carry over.

Example 4: Work out 78 X 89

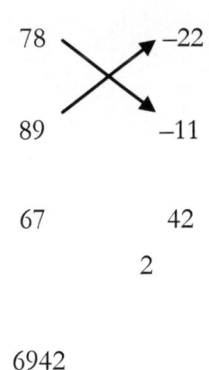

```
78          −22
    ╲    ╱
     ╲  ╱
      ╲╱
      ╱╲
     ╱  ╲
89          −11

67         42
        2
```

6942

Using crosswise subtraction we get 67. Using right hand column vertical multiplication we get 242 so we carry the 2 and put down the 42. The answer is thus 6942

Now try these questions yourself using base100.

Ex7A

(1) 96 X 95

(2) 88 X 92

(3) 78 X 92

(4) 102 X 108

(5) 106 X 104

(6) 95 X 85

(7) 87 X 93

(8) 95 X 95

(9) 112 X 118

This now completes methods of multiplication when working with bases up to 100. The pupil should now be familiar with base 10, base 20 and base 100.. In addition, we have also done the general case of crosswise and vertical multiplication for 2 digit numbers as well as the grid method of multiplication.

We will re-visit working with different bases and 3-digit multiplication later. The student should now begin to understand the basic principle of working to a given base appropriately. For example 9 X 8 or 12 X 13 may best be computed when with working to base 10. Whereas 98 X 89 or 97 X 93 would be more efficiently computed if worked out to base 100. On the other hand a sum such as 45 X 21 has numbers diversely different and it may be best worked out by vertical and crosswise multiplication or the grid method. The speed methods presented here do require practice just as any other system. The difference is the significant efficiency in the ease and speed of calculation that results from this system.

Chapter 8

Squaring Numbers between 11 & 19 with ease

By the time kids are 9 years old they should be introduced to squaring single digits and their notation.

Starting with single digit numbers, for example, 4^2 means $4 \times 4 = 16$, $5^2 = 5 \times 5 = 25$, $6^2 = 6 \times 6 = 36$, $7^2 = 7 \times 7 = 49$ and so on until 9^2 or 9×9.

Once they are ready to move on to double digit numbers, hopefully by the age of 9 or 10, then the fast method below will prove useful for them and will motivate them to learn more.

Example1:

Work out the square of 12

Step (1) gives us 14 (Take the last digit of 12 and add it to 12)

Step (2) Square the last digit of the original number. So $2 \times 2 = 4$

Step (3) Place this answer at the end of 14 in step (1) to get 144

So $12 \times 12 = 144$

Example 2:

Work out the square of 13.

Step (1) gives us 16 (Simply add the last digit to the number itself)

Step (2) gives us 9 (This was obtained by squaring the last digit of 13)

Step (3) gives us 169 (we simply place 9 at the end of 16)

So $13 \times 13 = 169$

Example 3:

Work out the square of 14.

Step (1) produces 18

Step (2) Produces 16

Step (3) Produces   18   6
                     1

(Carry the '1' to the 'tens' digit on the left)

That means 1 has now to be added to 18 to produce 196 as the final answer.

Example 4:

Work out the square of 15.

Step (1) produces 20

Step (2) Produces 25

Step (3) Produces   20   5

                              2

(Carry the '2' to the 'tens' digit on the left)

That means '2' has now to be added to 20 to produce 225 as the final answer.

See if you can work out the following:

Ex 8A

(1) 14 X 14
(2) 15 X 15
(3) 16 X 16
(4) 17 X 17
(5) 18 X 18
(6) 19 X 19

Chapter 9

Special case (1)

This is a very neat method of squaring numbers ending in 5 which children love. Useful from age 8 onwards.

Square numbers ending in 5

Note that squaring is simply multiplying a number itself.

15^2 means 15 X 15

Example 1: Work out 15 X 15

The answer has two parts. If the numbers to be multiplied each end in 5, then the last part is always 25. The first part is the first digit multiplied by 'one more'. In this case this is 1 X 2=2. So the first part is 2. The answer is thus 225.

Another two examples will help consolidate this method.

Example 2: Work out 25 X 25

As before, the answer has two parts. The last part is always 25. The first part is the first digit multiplied by 'one more'. In this case this is 2 X 3=6. So the first part is 6. The answer is thus 625

Example 3: Work out 65 X 65

The first part is 6 X 7=42 (Since the first digit is 6 and multiplying it by 'one more' makes it 6 X 7). The second part as before is 25. The answer is thus 4225

This method works with any two same digit numbers ending in 5. So for example 115 X 115

The answer has two parts. The last part is 25. The first part is 11 X 12 (first two digit number multiplied by 'one more'). The first part is thus 132. Hence, 115 X 115= 13225.

Try squaring a big number such as: 9995 X 9995

Last part is 25. The first part is 999 X 1000=999000. The answer is thus 99900025

Now try to work these out yourself.

Ex9A:
(1) 35 X 35

(2) 45 X 45

(3) 55 X 55

(4) 75 X 75

(5) 8.5 X 8.5

(6) 9.5 X 95

(7) 105 X 105

(8) 195 X 195

Special case (2)

Multiplication when all the digits before the last digit are the same and the last digits add up to 10. More advanced students will like these methods too. Useful for ages 9-11 years.

Example 1: Work out 32 X 38 (Notice the first digit for each number is the same and the last digits add up to 10)

As before the answer is in two parts. The last part is simply the last digit of each number multiplied together and the first part is the first digit multiplied by one more. In this case the last part is 2 X 8=16. The first part is 3 X 4=12. So the answer is 1216

Example 2: work out 56 X 54

(Note that the first digit of each part of the sum is the same, namely, 5 and the last digit of each part of the sum adds up to 10 that is 6+4=10)

The answer is in two parts. The last part is simply 6 X 4=24 and the first part is 5 times 'one more'. This makes it 5 X 6=30. Hence the answer is 3024

Three more examples will help consolidate this method.

Example 3: Work out 78 X 72

The last part is 8 X 2=16

The first part is 7 X 8=56 (first number times 'one more')

Hence the answer is 5616

Example 4: Work out 123 X 127

The last part is 3 X 7 =21

The first part is 12 X 13 (first number in this case is 12)=156

Hence the answer is 15621.

Example 5: Work out 9996 X 9994

The last part is 6 X 4=24

The first part is 999 X 1000=999000

Hence the answer is 99900024

We can see that this is a really powerful method of multiplication for this special case of numbers.

Practice questions:

Use a suitable method in each case.

Ex9B:
- (1) 93 X 97
- (2) 88 X 82
- (3) 67 X 63
- (4) 48 X 42
- (5) 83 X 87
- (6) 98 X 92
- (7) 122 X 128
- (8) 127 X 123
- (9) 118 X 112
- (10) 158 X 152
- (11) 167 X 163
- (12) 196 X 194
- (13) 402 X 408

Chapter 10

Division

In general the traditional short division approach is a good method. However, there are some other smart techniques worth considering for special situations.

Children at the age of 7 and 8 years should be able to halve even numbers. Dividing even numbers by 2 is a very useful skill. Children at 9 years plus will certainly need to be able to divide odd numbers by 2 as well. As they progress doing elementary division the methods below will also prove to be useful for special cases of division. Children who are 10 -11 years old as well as older children will find this chapter useful.

Dividing by 2, 4 and 8

Simply halve the number to divide by 2

(Some pupils find it difficult to halve a number like 13. An alternative strategy is to multiply the number by 5 and divide by 10)

Halving again is the same as dividing by 4

And halving once more is the same as dividing by 8

Example 1: $16 \div 2 = 8$

Example 2: $28 \div 2 = 14$

Example 3: $268 \div 4 = 134 \div 2 = 67$

Example 4: $568 \div 8 = 284 \div 4 = 142 \div 2 = 71$

Example 5: $65 \div 4 = 32.5 \div 2 = 16.25$

Dividing by 5

An easy way to do this is to multiply the number by 2 and divide by 10.

Example 1: $120 \div 5 = (120 \times 2) \div 10 = 240 \div 10 = 24$

Example 2: $127 \div 5 = (127 \times 2) \div 10 = 254 \div 10 = 25.4$

Example 3: $3432 \div 5 = (3432 \times 2) \div 10 = 6864 \div 10 = 686.4$

Similarly to divide by 50 simply multiply by 2 and divide by 100

Dividing by 25

A good way to do this is to multiply by 4 and divide by 100.

Example1: $240 \div 25 = (240 \times 4) \div 100 = 960 \div 100 = 9.6$

Example2: $700 \div 25 = (700 \times 4) \div 100 = 2800 \div 100 = 28$

Dividing by 9

Suppose we want to divide a 2-digit number by 9. The examples below will show the ease with which we can do these.

Example 1: Work out 12 divided by 9. Which is 12/9

Method: re-write the sum as shown.

    9 | 1/2 (split the 12 as 1 /2)

          /1 (bring the first digit of the dividend 12 to the right.)

      ————

    Answer is 1/3 (1 remainder 3)

We want to divide 12 by 9. Re-write as shown. Now bring the first number of the dividend sum to the right. Note the '1' vertically below 2. Now simply add the two rows on the right so we have 1/3 as the answer. Which means 1 remainder 3.

Example 2: Work out 31 /9

    9 | 3/1 (split the 31 as 3 /1)

        /3 (bring the first digit of the dividend 31 to the right)

————

Answer is 3/4 (3 remainder 4)

Example 3: Work out 42 /9

    9 | 4/2 (split the 42 as 4 /2)

        /4 (bring the first digit of the dividend 42 to the right)

————

Answer is 4/6 (4 remainder 6)

Example 4: Work out 53 /9

    9 | 5/3   (split the 53 as 5 /3)

          /5   (bring the first digit of the dividend 53 to the right)

———————

Answer is 5/8   (5 remainder 8)

We will now examine dividing 9 into 3 digit numbers:

Example 5: Work out 161 /9

    9 | 16/1   (split the 161 as 16 /1)

          1/7   (The first digit '1' is put as shown, also add the first two
                digits (1+6) and place as shown.)

———————

Answer is 17/8   17 remainder 8

You will notice in this case that 161 is split up as 16/1. Also the first digit is placed under the second digit and the sum of the first two digits is placed under the last digit as shown.

We then add the two rows as previously to get 17/8.

Two more examples will reinforce this method.

Example 6: Work out 103 /9

    9 | 10/3   (split the 103 as 10 /3)

          1/1   (The first digit '1' is put as shown, also add the first two
                digits (1+0) and place as shown.)

———————

Answer is 11/4   11 remainder 4

Example 7: Work out 521/9

```
9 | 52/1    (split the 521 as 52 /1)
    5/7
    57/8    (The first digit '5' is put as shown, also add the first two
             digits (5+2) and place as shown)
```

Answer is 57/8   57 remainder 8

Now we will consider division by 9 that requires a carry over

Also note that if the remainder is greater than the divisor, we can still do the division as before but then remember to carry the one to the left appropriately. The example below will attempt to show this.

Divide 138 by 9

```
9 | 13/8    (split the 138 as 13 /8)

    1/4     (The first digit '1' is put as shown, also add the first two
             digits (1+3) and place as shown.)
```

This gives 14/12 (14 remainder 12)

Answer is actually 15/3

Now since 12 is more than 9. We can still divide by 9 again. This gives us a remainder of 3 and a carry 1 to the left hand side. The answer is thus 15/3

Another example with a carry over will consolidate this process.
Work out 237/9

$$9 \,\Big|\, 23/7 \quad \text{(split the 237 as 23 /7)}$$

$$2/5 \quad \text{(The first digit '2' is put as shown, also add the first two digits (2+3) and place as shown.)}$$

This gives 25/12 (25 remainder 12)

Actual answer is 26/3

Dividing by 11

A smart strategy to work this out is to write down the first digit under the second digit and subtract, write this answer under the third digit and subtract until the last digit.

Example 1: 561 ÷ 11

$$5\ 6\ 1$$
$$5\ 1$$

Notice the first digit is placed under the second digit, after subtraction the answer is placed under the final digit. Since subtraction now gives zero there is no remainder.

Example 2: 56787 ÷ 11

$$5\ 6\ 7\ 8\ 7$$
$$5\ 1\ 6\ 2\ r5$$

The answer is 5162, remainder 5

Chapter 11

Fractions, decimal and percentage equivalents

Most pupils by the time they are 9 years plus should be aware that ½ is equal to 0.5. This in turn is equal to 50%.

It is worth reviewing this fact. In addition they should try and remember the following other equivalences: This chapter will be useful for children between 9 and 11 years of age, although experience shows that many older children will benefit too!

Fractions	Decimal	Percentage
$\dfrac{1}{2}$	0.5	50%
$\dfrac{1}{4}$	0.25	25%
$\dfrac{3}{4}$	0.75	75%
$\dfrac{1}{10}$	0.1	10%

If necessary remind your children what a half, quarter, three quarters and a tenth means – you can use the diagram below or show them a diagram of cutting cakes in halves, quarters, a third or in ten pieces!

(1) The example below shows the meaning of a half. In this case half of the diagram is crossed.

(2) In this case one third or 1/3 of the diagram is crossed

(3) Finally in the diagram below one tenth or 1/10 is crossed.

So children should now understand fractions conceptually.

If, we know $\dfrac{1}{2} = 0.5$

We can deduce that $\dfrac{1}{4} = 0.25$

(Since a quarter is half of half)

Similarly $\dfrac{1}{8}$ is **0.125**

We can do this quickly because all we do is halve each decimal value.

Half of 0.5 is 0.25

Half of 0.25 is 0.125

We can of course continue this process.

Further if we know $\dfrac{1}{10} = 0.1$ **we can now work out** $\dfrac{2}{10}, \dfrac{3}{10}, \dfrac{7}{10}$ etc.

$\dfrac{2}{10} = 0.2$ **(2 X 0.1)**

$\dfrac{3}{10} = 0.3$

$\dfrac{7}{10} = 0.7$

$\dfrac{9}{10} = 0.9$

By extension the equivalent percentages are as follows:

$\frac{1}{2} = 50\%$

$\frac{1}{4} = 25\%$

$\frac{1}{8} = 12.5\%$

$\frac{1}{16} = 6.25\%$

Summary

Get kids to remember

$\frac{1}{2} = 0.5 = 50\%$, $\frac{1}{4} = 0.25 = 25\%$, $\frac{3}{4} = 0.75 = 75\%$, and $\frac{1}{10} = 0.1 = 10\%$

This will help them work out many other decimal and percentage equivalents.

Example 1: Find 25% of £250

Method: Find 50% of £250 and halve it again.
Half of £250 = £125
Half of £125 = £62.50

Example 2:
Find 12.5% of £800
Method:
Now, 50% = £400 (This is half of £800)
So, 25% = £200 (This is half of £400)
Finally, 12.5% = £100 (This is half of £200)

Example 3:

Find 75% of £600

Method:

First find 50% = £300

Then find 25% = £150

Total 75% = £450

Example 4:

I buy an apartment for $150,000. After two years, I make a profit of 20%. What is the new selling price?

Find 20% of $150,000. Using the methods above this works out to $30,000

Hence the new selling price is the old price plus profit. So the new selling price is $150,000+$30,000 =$180,000

Example 5:

I buy a coat at a discount of 20% and pay £60. What was the original price?

Method: If I pay 20% less it means I pay 80% of the price.

If 80% costs £60 then 1% costs £60 ÷ 80

Hence, 100% (the original price) is $£\dfrac{60}{80} \times 100 = £\dfrac{6}{8} \times 100 = £\dfrac{600}{8}$

$£\dfrac{600}{8} = £\dfrac{300}{4} = £\dfrac{150}{2} = £75$

So, the original price is £75

Example 6:

I have $1000 in a savings account that earns 5% per annum compound interest. How much will I have at the end of two years?

Method: At the end of the first year I will have $1000 plus 5% of $1000 =$1000 plus $50 =$1050

So, at the end of the second year I will have $1050 plus 5% of $1050

Since 10% of $1050 =$105, 5% =$52.50

So the total at the end of the second year is $1050 +$52.50 =$1102.50

Summary:

To work out any percent that cannot be derived easily use the method shown below:

You need to remember that 1 percent means 1 out of 100. That is $\frac{1}{100}$. So to find say 42.5% first find 1% and multiply it by 42.5.

Example work out 42.5% of $400

We can say that this is the same as ($400 ÷ 100) X 42.5 = 4 X 42.5 = $170

What about the use of calculators?

Yes, of course children should use their calculators if, for example, they need to work out 45.67% of £3456! However, for most every day questions they should rarely need it! (E.g. when asked to work out 10%, 50%, 25% or 75%)

For the exercise below, you may use your calculators to work out the answers to questions 10 and 11 if you need to!

Try these.

Ex11A:

(1) Find 50% of $550

(2) Find 25% of £500

(3) Find 30% of $800

(4) Find 15% of $300

(5) Find 75% of £1200

(6) Find 0.5 of $300

(7) Find 0.25 of £400

(8) Find 0.75 of $900

(9) 70% of $8000

(10) 42.2% of $5670

(11) 89.15% of $6578

(12) I buy a car for £6000 and sell it two years later at a loss of 40%. What is my selling price?

(13) I buy a shirt in a sale, which is reduced by 25%. The price I pay is £15. What is the original price?

Chapter 12

Number Sequences

Many numerical aptitude tests contain questions involving identifying number patterns in order to find the subsequent missing number(s). Although some of these are hard they will be useful to 11 year olds preparing for various entrance exams.

Try these questions yourself and see how many you can do. Then check the answers and their rationale. See if you can improve your score in the subsequent test.

Complete the following sequences by finding the missing numbers:

(1) 4, 7, 10, 13, ___ , ___

(2) 21, 17, 13, 9, 5, ___ , ___

(3) 18, 9, 4.5, ___ , ___

(4) 0, 1, 1, 2, 3, 5, 8, ___ , ___

(5) 1, 4, 9, 16, 25, ___ , ___

(6) 1, 8, 27, 64, ___ , ___

(7) 17, 12, 7, 2, ___ , ___

(8) 1, 6, 36, 216, ___ , ___

(9) 128, 32, 8, ___ , ___

(10) 36, 49, 64, 81, ___ , ___

(11) 11, 121, 1331, ___ , ___

(12) 0.142857, 0.285714, 0.428571, ___ , ___

(13) 81, 729, 6561, ___ , ___

(14) 1, 3, 6, 10, ___ , ___

Answers and their rationale:

(1) 16, 19 (each number increases by a constant value of 3)

(2) 1, -3 (each number decreases by a constant value of 4)

(3) 2.25, 1.125 (each number is half the previous number)

(4) 13, 21 (each number is the sum of the previous two numbers)

(5) 36, 49 (each number is the square of natural numbers, the first number is 1 X 1, the second number is 2 X 2, the third number is 3 X 3, ...the sixth number is 6 X 6, the seventh number is 7 X 7)

(6) 343, 512 (cubes of natural numbers. The first number is 1 X 1 X 1, the second number is 2 X 2 X 2, 3 X 3 X 3, ...7 X 7 X 7, 8 X 8 X 8)

(7) –3, -8 (numbers are decreasing by 5)

(8) 1296, 7776 (each number is 6X the previous number)

(9) 2, 1/2 (each number is a quarter of the previous number)

(10) 100, 121 (square numbers again, the previous number was 9 X 9, then 10 X 10 and finally 11 X 11)

(11) 14641, 161051 (each number is 11X the previous number)

(12) 0.571428, 0.714285 (these numbers are cyclic numbers each preceding starting number being the lower in the series)

(13) 59049, 531441 (each number is 9X the previous one)

(14) 15, 21 (Triangular numbers, the last difference was 5 and the subsequent 6.)

Ex 12A (with hints)

(1) 7, 12, 17, ___, ___ (Increase each number by 5,)
(2) 16, 25, 36, ___, ___ (Square the numbers in progression)
(3) 1, 11, 121, ___, ___ (Multiply the previous number by 11)
(4) 0, 1, 1, 2, 3, 5, ___, ___ (Next number is sum of previous two)
(5) 50, 25, 12.5, ___, ___ (Halve the previous number)
(6) 18, 13, 8, 3, ___, ___ (Decrease each number by 5)
(7) 5, 25, 125, ___, ___ (Next number is 5X previous number)
(8) 64, 16, 4, ___, ___ (Next number is a quarter of previous one)
(9) 1, 9, 81, ___, ___ (next number is 9X previous number)

Now try a similar number sequence test:

Ex12B:

(1) 11, 16, 21, ___, ___
(2) 49, 64, 81, ___, ___
(3) 2, 22, 242, ___, ___
(4) 5, 11, 17, ___, ___
(5) 60, 30, 15, ___, ___
(6) 16, 11, 8, 3, ___, ___
(7) 4, 16, 64, ___, ___
(8) 1600, 400, 100, ___, ___
(9) 1, 7, 49, ___, ___

Finding the Nth term of a sequence:

Example 1:
Consider the sequence 2, 4, 6, 8, 10, ___ , ___ , ___ ,

If we want to find a general formula for this sequence we can write it as 2n.

2n is the right answer, since if n=1, we get 2 as the first number. If n=2, we get 2 X 2 =4 as the second number, if n=4, we get 8 as the fourth number and so on. All we have to do is to substitute the appropriate number for n to get the relevant number in the sequence. So the 50th term is 2 X 50 =100.

Example 2:
Consider a general arithmetical sequence as shown:

a, a +d, a+2d, a +3d, a+4d, a+5d, a+6d, ...

We can see that the second term is a+d

The third term is a+2d

The fourth term is a+3d

The fifth term is a+4d or a +(5-1)d

The sixth term is a+5d or a +(6-1)d

The seventh term is a+6d or a +(7-1)d

So the nth term is a+(n-1)d

You can check to see if this is right by substituting n=1, 2, 3, 4, 5 and so on to the appropriate numbers in the sequence.

Example 3:
5, 9, 13, 17

This is an arithmetical or linear sequence since the numbers go up by the same constant number.

We know the nth term is a +(n-1)d

In this case a=5 (This is the first term)

d = 4 (this is the common difference between each successive number)

So, the nth term is 5+(n - 1) X 4

=5 +4n −4

=4n +1

Example 5:

Find the nth term of the following sequence:

2, 4, 8, 16, 32, ___ , ___ , ...

A common mistake is to say the nth term is 2n! If this were right then accordingly, the third term should be 6 and the fourth term 8. But you can see from the sequence that this is not the case. The answer is 2^n, which reads 2 to the power 'n'. So the second term is 2 X 2, the third term is 2 X 2 X 2, the fourth term, is 2 X 2 X 2 X 2 and so on

Example 6:

Consider the triangular numbers below:

1, 3, 6, 10, 15, 21 ___ , ___

The nth term in this case is n(n+1)/2

Example 7:

Find the nth term of the square numbers as shown:

1, 4, 9, 16, 25, 36, 49, ___ , ___ , ...

The nth term is n^2

Example 8:

Find the nth term of the cubic numbers below:

1, 8, 27, 64, 125, ___ , ___ , ...

In this case the nth term is n^3

Chapter 13

Estimating

Estimating is a very important skill and the sooner children can learn it the better. Starting at 9 years of age and re-visiting periodically at 10, 11 12 and even in the early teens is a good idea.

We will start simply with rounding numbers to the nearest 10 and 100

Consider the number 271

Rounded to the nearest 10 this number is 270

Rounded to the nearest 100 this number is 300

(The principle is that if the right hand digit is lower than 5 you drop this number and replace it by 0. Conversely if the number is 5 or more drop that digit and add 1 to the left)

Try a few more:

Round 5,382 to the nearest 10, 100 & 1000

5,382 to the nearest 10 is 5380

5,382 to the nearest hundred is 5,400

5,382 to the nearest 1000 is 5000

This rule can also be applied to decimal numbers:

Round 3.7653 to the nearest thousandth, hundredth, tenth and nearest unit.

3.7653 rounded to the nearest thousandth is 3.765

3.7653 rounded to the nearest hundredth is 3.77

3.7653 rounded to the nearest tenth is 3.8

3.7653 rounded to the nearest unit is 4

Now try these yourself.

Ex13A:

(1) **Round the following numbers to the nearest 10**
- (a) 432
- (b) 563
- (c) 4678
- (d) 52
- (e) 6,753
- (f) 6,666

(2) **Round the following numbers to the nearest 100**
- (a) 4,567
- (b) 6,548
- (c) 643
- (d) 210
- (e) 2,345
- (f) 6,578

(3) **Round the following numbers to the nearest 1000**
- (a) 56,432
- (b) 56,321
- (c) 64,020
- (d) 65,431
- (e) 11,234
- (f) 123,456

(4) **Round the following numbers to the nearest tenth**
- (a) 45.34334
- (b) 12.523
- (c) 1.089
- (d) 123.587

(5) Round the following numbers to the nearest unit
   (a) 1.256
   (b) 3.67
   (c) 0.87
   (d) .001

For smarter 10 and 11 year olds this is not too difficult. Consider Significant Figures (s.f.)

Normally, the first digit is the first significant figure except when it is 0, when you do not count it. Remember to get the size of the number right when working out significant figures.

Ex1: Write 53.6 to 1 s.f.

Answer is 50 (It is not 5)

Ex2: Write 262.7 to 2 s.f.

Answer is 260 (It is not 26)

Ex3: Write 0.0384 to 1 s.f.

Answer is 0.04 (ignore the 0 at the beginning)

Remember to get the right size of the answer by following the usual rules of rounding.

How can, rounding help in estimating your answers?

Say you want to multiply 187 X 9

You know the answer is less than 190 X 10, which is 1900. This immediately gives you an idea of how big the answer is. It may not be the actual answer, but it gives you an indication of the magnitude of the answer.

Some more examples will help:
   Example 1: Work out (2.2 X 7.12)/4.12
   We can quickly estimate that this is roughly equal to (2 X 7)/4
   =14/4 which is around 3.5 or 4 rounded to the nearest unit.
   The actual answer is: 3.8 (to 1 decimal place)
   You can see our estimate gave us a very good idea of the size of the answer.

   Example 2: Work out 38 X 2.9 X 0.53

We can approximate 38 to be 40 to the nearest ten

We can approximate 2.9 o 3 to the nearest unit

We can approximate 0.53 to 0.5 to the nearest tenth

So the magnitude of the answer is 40 X 3 X 0.5

Which is 120 X 0.5 = 60 (approximately)

The actual answer is 58.406

Estimation is very important in practice as we obtain a guide to the size of an answer very quickly. Consider a practical example as shown below:

Example 3:

Estimate the total bill at an American super market with the following price tags:

	Real price	Rounded price	Cumulative total
Milk	$.93	$1	$1
Cheese	$2.10	$2	$3
Lettuce	$1.05	$1	$4
Bread	$1.95	$2	$6
Coffee	$1.45	$1.50	$7.50

Total real price: $7.48

Estimated price: $7.50

You may not always get as close as this, but you should have a very good idea of the size of the answer.

Chapter 14

Multiplication revisited

Base 1000

We are now familiar with multiplying numbers near to a given base. Let us try a few examples near base 1000.

Example 1: Work out 892 X 998

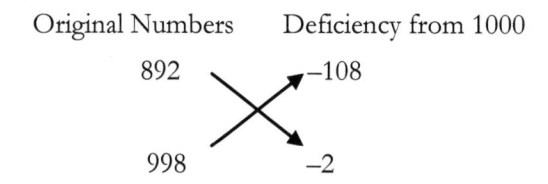

Original Numbers   Deficiency from 1000

```
    892           -108
       ╲        ╱
        ╳
       ╱        ╲
    998           -2
```

Using the usual rules of cross subtraction and vertical multiplication we get the result below:

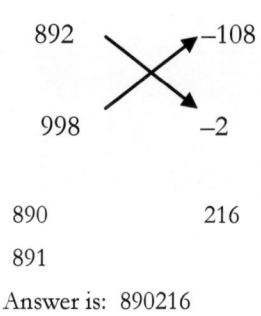

```
    892           -108
       ╲        ╱
        ╳
       ╱        ╲
    998           -2

    890           216
    891
```

Answer is: 890216

Example 2: Work out 987 X 992

```
    987           -13
       ╲        ╱
        ╳
       ╱        ╲
    992           -8

    979           104
```

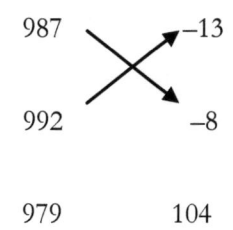

65

Using the usual rules of cross subtraction and vertical multiplication and we get the result as shown.

A few more examples will help us understand this elegant and rapid process.

Example 3: Work out 850 X 996

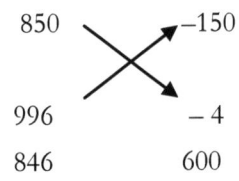

```
    850          −150
        ╲    ╱
         ╳
        ╱    ╲
    996          − 4
    846          600
```

The answer in this case is 846600

We will now look at an example where the numbers are above 1000 in both cases.

Example 4: Work out 1021 X 1030

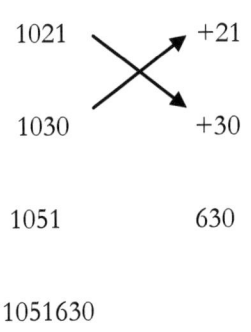

```
   1021          +21
        ╲    ╱
         ╳
        ╱    ╲
   1030          +30

   1051          630
```

1051630

Remember from previous chapters on base arithmetic this time we cross add instead of cross subtracting. This gives us 1051 as the first part of the answer.

The second part as per vertical multiplication of the right hand column is 630. So the answer is 1051630 as shown.

What about situations where we cannot work appropriately with a base as the numbers are diversely different from the base?

Fortunately, we have a technique for 3 X 3 digits. This can then be expanded to 'N X N' digits. This technique is similar to the technique we met earlier for working out 2 X 2 multiplications. The next chapter will demonstrate this.

Chapter 15

General approach to 3 X 3 multiplication

This chapter is for **smart 11 year olds and beyond.** Some children might prefer conventional techniques, such as standard long multiplication or the grid method introduced earlier and this is fine. Whatever works and brings excitement is the way forward.

Let us assume we want to multiply two 3 digit numbers abc and def together.

(Do not worry if you find the general case difficult to follow. Once we do some actual examples you will see how easy it actually is.)

The steps required are shown below.

Problem: Multiply two, three digit numbers abc by def.

The multiplication is done vertically and crosswise as you learnt earlier for the 2 X 2 multiplication. The full process will now be explored. Note that there are five parts to the answer as shown.

Step 1: Re-write question as shown. The first and the last part of the answer is found by vertical multiplication as shown.

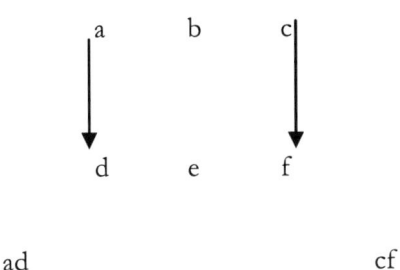

```
        a       b       c
        |               |
        ↓               ↓
        d       e       f

    ad                      cf
```

The first part of the answer is ad. The last part is cf as shown.

(The first is obtained by multiplying a X d and the last part by multiplying c X f)

Step 2: Draw arrows as shown.

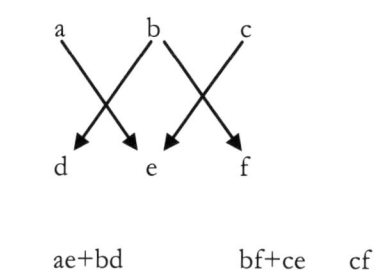

$$\begin{matrix} a & b & c \\ & \times\times & \\ d & e & f \end{matrix}$$

ad   ae+bd   bf+ce   cf

The second part of the answer is found by multiplying the next two digits crosswise and adding. This is shown by the arrows, that is ae + bd. Likewise the fourth part is found by multiplying crosswise and adding the last two digits as shown by the arrows. That is bf + ce.

We now have only the middle part to find.

Step 3: To find the middle part, follow the arrows as shown.

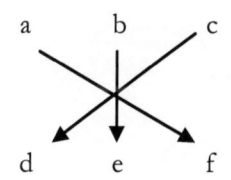

$$\begin{matrix} a & b & c \\ & \times & \\ d & e & f \end{matrix}$$

ad   ae+bd   <u>af+cd+be</u>   bf+ce   cf

The middle part is the underlined bit, which is: af + cd + be

This general example may seem a bit strange if you are not familiar with algebra. However, the next few examples will help clarify how simple the actual process is.

Example 1: Work out 122 X 311

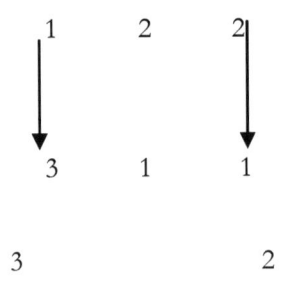

```
1   2   2
|   |   |
v   v   v
3   1   1

3           2
```

So the first part of the answer is 3X1=3 and the last part is 2X1=2.

Now consider the second part and the fourth part of the answer.

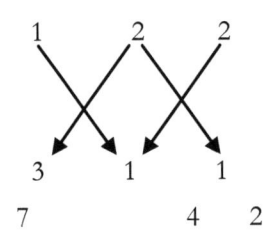

```
    1   2   2
     \ / \ /
      X   X
     / \ / \
    3   1   1
3   7       4   2
```

The second part is 1 X 1+ 2 X 3=7 as shown by the arrows. Likewise the fourth part is 2 X 1+2 X 1 =4.

Now we need to find the middle part.

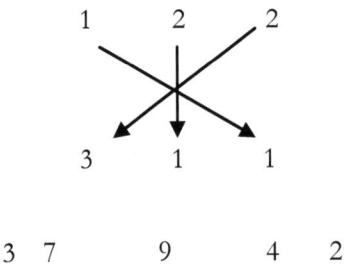

```
    1   2   2
     \  |  /
      \ | /
       \|/
       /|\
      / | \
     /  |  \
    3   1   1

3   7   9   4   2
```

By following the arrows we have the middle part as 1 X 1 + 2 X 3 + 2 X 1 = 9
The answer is thus 37942. Although the method took a long time to explain with a little practice you will find this approach a very efficient method to use.

Example 2: Work out 213 X 123

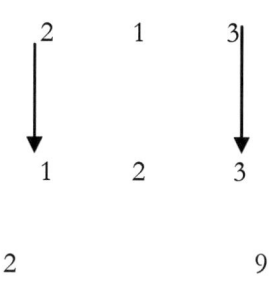

So the first part of the answer is 2 X 1=2 and the last part is 3 X 3=9.

Now consider the second part and the fourth part of the answer.

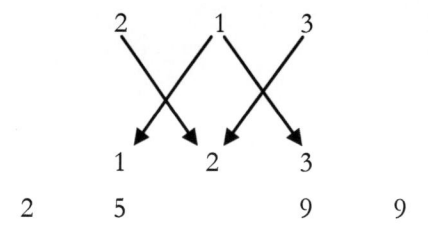

The second part is 2 X 2 + 1 X 1 =5 as shown by the arrows. Likewise the fourth part is 1 X 3+3 X 2 = 9.

Finally, we need to find the middle part.

```
    2   1   3
     ╲ │ ╱
      ╳
     ╱ │ ╲
    1   2   3

  2  5      1      9   9
          1
```

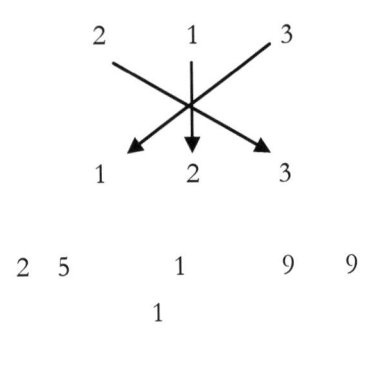

26199

The middle part is thus 2 X 3 +3 X 1 +1 X 2 =11. Because we have 11(two digits) as the answer we put down the 1 and carry the 1. This gives us the answer 26199 as shown.

One more example will help us consolidate this method.

Example 3: Work out 213 X 314

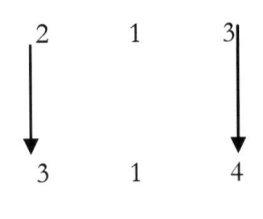

```
    2   1   3
    │   │   │
    ▼   ▼   ▼
    3   1   4


         6              2
                    1
```

By vertical multiplication the first and the last part of the answer is 1 and 12 respectively. Notice we put down the 2 and carry the 1 as shown.

Now consider the second part and the fourth part of the answer.

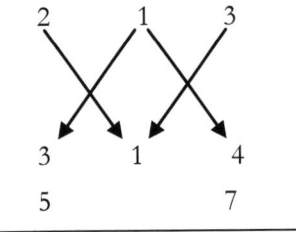

```
       2   1   3
        ╲ ╱ ╲ ╱
         ╳   ╳
        ╱ ╲ ╱ ╲
       3   1   4
    6   5       7   2
```

The second part is 2 X 1 + 1 X 3 = 5 as shown by the arrows. Likewise the fourth part is 3 X 1 +1 X 4 =7

Now we need to find the middle part.

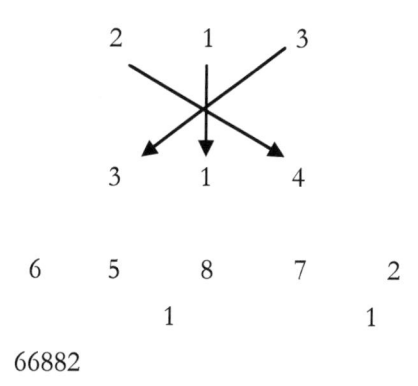

```
    2     1     3
         ╲│╱
         ╱│╲
    3     1     4

  6    5    8    7    2
            1         1
 66882
```

The middle part is thus 2 X 4 +3 X 3 +1 X 1 =18. Because we have 18(two digits) as the answer we put down the 8 and carry the 1. This gives us the answer

66882 as shown.

Summary:
You simply use the vertical and crosswise multiplication rule as shown above. If you need to multiply a 3 digit number by a 2 digit number just put a zero before the 2 digit number and carry out the same operations. Example 234 X 51 can be re-written as 234 X 051.

The algebraic proof for those interested is as follows:

$ax^2 +bx +c$

$\underline{dx^2 +ex +f}$

$\overline{adx^4 +(ae+bd)x^3+(af+be+cd)x^2+(bf+ce)x+cf}$

(Replace, x^2 with 10^2 and so on)

Now try these yourself using vertical and crosswise multiplication.

Ex15A:

(1) 213 X 111
(2) 322 X 223
(3) 412 X 132
(4) 321 X 452
(5) 611 X 521
(6) 801 X 902
(7) 566 X 23
(8) 675 X 87
(9) 511 X 611
(10) 75 X 123

Chapter 16

Fractions

A fraction is simply a part of a whole number. We have already met fractions such as, ½, ¼, ¾, and others. The top part of a fraction is called the numerator and the bottom part is called a denominator. The fraction is really a type of division so ½ means 1 divided by 2. This chapter will prove useful for 10 and 11 year olds. The later parts will also be useful for older kids.

We will now consider adding and subtracting fractions together.

Example1: Work out $\frac{1}{2} + \frac{2}{5}$

The traditional method of doing this is to find the common denominator.

We have to find a number that both 2 and 5 will go into. This is clearly 10.

We can now re-write the fraction with the same common denominator.

To do this we have to ask how did we get the denominator from 2 to 10 for the first part, and likewise for the second part from 5 to 10. The answer is shown below:

$$\frac{1 \times 5}{2 \times 5} + \frac{2 \times 2}{5 \times 2} = \frac{5}{10} + \frac{4}{10} = \frac{9}{10}$$

We had to multiply top and bottom by 5 for the first part and top and bottom by 2 for the second part as shown above. We can then add the fraction as we have the same common denominator.

We can however use another very simple strategy that always works. You guessed it right. The method is that of crosswise multiplication.

The basic method is to take the fraction sum and do crosswise multiplication as shown by the arrows. In addition multiply the denominators together to get the new denominator.

Take the fraction $\frac{1}{2} + \frac{2}{5}$ = $\frac{1 \times 5 + 2 \times 2}{10}$ = $\frac{5+4}{10}$ = $\frac{9}{10}$

We notice that if we cross multiply as shown we get 1 X 5 and 2 X 2 respectively at the top. To get the bottom number simply multiply the bottom numbers, 2 and 5 together. So the denominator is 2 X 5=10.

Let us try another example:

Example2: Work out $\dfrac{3}{7} + \dfrac{2}{5}$

Using crosswise multiplication and adding rule, as well as multiplying the bottom two numbers we get:

$$\dfrac{3 \times 2}{7 \quad 5} = \dfrac{3 \times 5 + 7 \times 2}{35} = \dfrac{15+14}{35} = \dfrac{29}{35}$$

This is a very elegant method that always works.

Example3: Work out $\dfrac{3}{7} - \dfrac{2}{5}$

This is similar to the above except instead of adding we now subtract as shown below.

$$\dfrac{3 \quad 2}{7 \quad 5} = \dfrac{3 \times 5 - 7 \times 2}{35} = \dfrac{15 - 14}{35} = \dfrac{1}{35}$$

Example 4: Work out $\dfrac{4}{7} + \dfrac{1}{2}$

Using crosswise multiplication we get the result as shown:

$$\dfrac{4 \times 1}{7 \quad 2} = \dfrac{2 \times 4 + 7 \times 1}{7 \times 2} = \dfrac{8 + 7}{14} = \dfrac{15}{14}$$

Notice the answer $\dfrac{15}{14}$, can be simplified further. 15/14 = $1\dfrac{1}{14}$

Now try to work out these yourself.

Ex16A:

(1) 2/5 + 1/4
(2) 2/7 + 1/8
(3) 1/3 + 5/6
(4) 1/7 + 3/5
(5) 2/9 + 1/4
(6) 2/3 – 1/7
(7) 4/7 – 1/8
(8) 5/11 – 3/12
(9) 7/13 – 8/5
(10) 3/16 – 2/11

Adding and subtracting mixed numbers:

This is a similar process. We first add or subtract the whole numbers and then the fractional parts.

Ex1: $2\dfrac{2}{5} + 4\dfrac{3}{7}$

Adding the whole numbers we get 6. (Simply add 2 and 4)

Now add the fractional parts to get: $\dfrac{14+15}{35} = \dfrac{29}{35}$

So the answer is $6\dfrac{29}{35}$

Ex2: $4\dfrac{3}{7} - 2\dfrac{2}{5}$

Subtract the whole numbers and then the fractional parts, which gives us:

$2\dfrac{15-14}{35} = 2\dfrac{1}{35}$

Now try these yourself.

Ex16B:

(1) $2\dfrac{1}{5} + 4\dfrac{3}{8}$

(2) $6\dfrac{1}{3} + 4\dfrac{3}{7}$

(3) $3\dfrac{2}{9} + 2\dfrac{3}{11}$

(3) $7\dfrac{4}{5} - 4\dfrac{3}{7}$

(4) $8\dfrac{2}{11} - 3\dfrac{1}{13}$

Multiplying Fractions

Multiplying fractions by the traditional method is quite efficient so we will consider only this approach.

Example 1: $\dfrac{2}{3} \times \dfrac{5}{7} = \dfrac{10}{21}$

In this case we simply multiply the top two numbers to get the new numerator and multiply the bottom two numbers together to get the new denominator, as shown above.

Another example will help consolidate this process:

Example 2: $\dfrac{10}{21} \times \dfrac{5}{7} = \dfrac{50}{147}$

(Multiply 10 X 5 to get 50 for the numerator and 21 X 7 to get 147 for the denominator)

Division of Fractions

When dividing fractions we invert the second fraction and multiply as shown.

Think of an obvious example. If we have to divide ½ by ¼ we intuitively know that the answer is 2. The reason for this is that there are 2 quarters in one half. Let us see how this works in practice.

Example 1: $\dfrac{1}{2} \div \dfrac{1}{4} = \dfrac{1}{2} \times \dfrac{4}{1} = \dfrac{4}{2} = 2$

Step 1: Re-write fraction as a multiplication sum with the second fraction inverted.

Step 2: Work out the fraction as a normal multiplication

Step 3: Simplify if possible. In this case 4 divided by 2 is 2.

Let us try a harder example.

Example 2: $\dfrac{3}{5} \div \dfrac{2}{7} = \dfrac{3}{5} \times \dfrac{7}{2} = \dfrac{21}{10} = 2$ remainder 1

2, remainder 1 can be written as $2\dfrac{1}{10}$ (Since the remainder is divided by 10, the denominator of the fraction)

We will do one more example to see how simple this process is.

Example 3: $\dfrac{6}{11} \div \dfrac{5}{11} = \dfrac{6}{11} \times \dfrac{11}{5} = \dfrac{66}{55} = \dfrac{6}{5} = 1\dfrac{1}{5}$

Step1: Re-write the fraction inverting the second fraction as shown

Step2: Multiply the top part and the bottom part to get $\dfrac{66}{55}$ **as shown.**

Step 3: Simplify this by dividing top and bottom by 11 to get $\dfrac{6}{5}$. **Now this finally simplifies to** $1\dfrac{1}{5}$ **as shown.**

(If you noticed you could have cancelled earlier, by dividing by 11 in the second part of the sum to give $\dfrac{6}{5}$ straight away. That is $\dfrac{6}{\cancel{11}} \times \dfrac{\cancel{11}}{5} = \dfrac{6}{5}$

Converting a mixed number to a fraction

A mixed number such as $2\frac{1}{4}$ can be re-written as $\frac{9}{4}$.

The following steps are required to convert a mixed number into a fraction.

Step 1: Multiply the denominator of the fractional part by the whole number and add the numerator. In this case this works out to 2 X 4 + 1 = 9. This now becomes the new numerator.

Step 2: The new denominator stays the same as before. Now re-write the new fraction as $\frac{9}{4}$. (That is the new numerator ÷ existing denominator)

Let us look at another example. Convert the mixed number, $3\frac{3}{7}$ into a fraction.

Step 1: Multiply denominator of fractional part by whole number and add the numerator. This gives 3 X 7+3 = 24 as the new numerator.

Step2: Re-write fraction as new fraction. This is now the new numerator ÷ existing denominator. This gives us $\frac{24}{7}$.

Multiplying a mixed numbers together

Consider the examples below:

Example 1: $1\frac{1}{5}$ X $1\frac{3}{8}$

The method is simply to convert both mixed numbers into fractions and multiply as shown below:

$$1\frac{1}{5} \times 1\frac{3}{8} = \frac{6}{5} \times \frac{11}{8} = \frac{66}{40} = 1\frac{26}{40} = 1\frac{13}{20}$$

(Notice $\frac{26}{40}$ simplifies to $\frac{13}{20}$)

Example 2: $1\frac{1}{3} \times 2\frac{2}{5}$

As before, convert the mixed numbers into fractions and multiply as shown.

$$1\frac{1}{3} \times 2\frac{2}{5} = \frac{4}{3} \times \frac{12}{5} = \frac{48}{15} = 3\frac{3}{15} = 3\frac{1}{5}$$

Dividing mixed numbers together

Example 1: $1\frac{1}{2} \div 1\frac{1}{4}$

There are two steps required to work out the division of mixed numbers.

Step 1: Convert both mixed numbers into fractions as before

Step 2: Multiply the fractions together but invert the second one.

$$1\frac{1}{2} \div 1\frac{1}{4} = \frac{3}{2} \div \frac{5}{4} = \frac{3}{2} \times \frac{4}{5} = \frac{12}{10} = 1\frac{2}{10} = 1\frac{1}{5}$$

Example 2: $2\frac{1}{3} \div 1\frac{1}{4}$

Following the same process as above, we have:

$$2\frac{1}{3} \div 1\frac{1}{4} = \frac{7}{3} \div \frac{5}{4} = \frac{7}{3} \times \frac{4}{5} = \frac{28}{15} = 1\frac{13}{15}$$

Now try these.

Ex16C:

(1) $2\frac{3}{7} \times 1\frac{1}{2}$

(2) $3\frac{3}{4} \times 1\frac{1}{2}$

(3) $4\dfrac{2}{3} \times 1\dfrac{1}{2}$

(4) $2\dfrac{3}{4} \div 1\dfrac{1}{2}$

(5) $3\dfrac{3}{5} \div 1\dfrac{1}{5}$

(6) $2\dfrac{2}{7} \div 1\dfrac{1}{7}$

Chapter 17

Proportions and ratios

Although proportion and ratio are related they are not the same thing. Consider the rectangle below where 3 parts out of 10 are shaded:

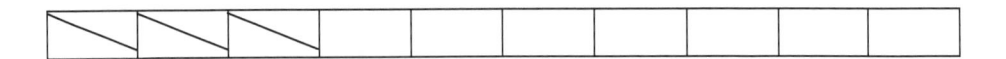

In this case the proportion of the rectangle that is shaded is $\frac{3}{10}$.

However, the ratio of the shaded part to the non-shaded part is 3 : 7

Consider the following examples.

Example 1:

$100 is divided in the ratio 1 : 4 how much is the bigger part?

The total number of parts that $100 is divided into is 5 (to find the number of parts simply add the numbers in the ratio, which in this case is 1 and 4)

Clearly, 1 part equals $20 (100 divided by 5)

So, 4 parts is equal to $80. This is the required bigger part.

Example 2:

$1500 is divided in the ratio of the 3 :5 :7

Find out how much the smallest part is worth?

Clearly $1500 is divided into a total of 15 Parts

So each part is worth $100 ($1500 divided by 15)

So, 3 parts (this is the smallest part) equals $300

Example 3:

Two lengths are in the ratio 3 : 5. If the first length is 150m what is the second length?

If the ratio is 3 : 5 then the lengths are in the ratio 150 : n

We now need to determine n. We can see that 150 is 50 times 3.

So, n (which is the second length) must be 50 times 5, which equals 250m.

Example 4:

Sometimes ratios are expressed in ways, which may not be the simplest form.

Consider 5 : 10

(a) You can re-write 5 : 10 as 1 : 2 (divide both sides by 5)

    (b) 4 : 10 can be re-written as 2 : 5

    (c) 8 : 60 can be re-written as 4 : 30 which, simplifies to 2 : 15

    (d) 15 : 36 simplifies to 5 : 12 (divide both sides by 3)

Now try these:

Ex17A:

(1) John and Ben share $500 between them in the ratio of 2 : 3. Find out how much each person gets?

(2) 90 kg is divided in the ratio 1: 8. Find out the largest part.

(3) The width and the length of the room are in the ratio 2 : 3

What is the length of the room if the width is 4.5m?

Chapter 18

Square Roots and Cube Roots:

The square root is written like this $\sqrt{}$ and means finding a number which when multiplied by itself, gives you the number inside the square root. The square root concept can be introduced at 9 years of age and certainly by 10!

Example1: Find $\sqrt{16}$. The answer is clearly 4. Since 4X4 =16

Let us consider some other square roots.

$\sqrt{25} = 5$

$\sqrt{36} = 6$

$\sqrt{49} = 7$

$\sqrt{121} = 11$

$\sqrt{100} = 10$

Now try these.

Ex18A:

(Hint! Try and guess a number which when multiplied by itself gives you the number inside the square root.)

(1) $\sqrt{81}$

(2) $\sqrt{144}$

(3) $\sqrt{64}$

(4) $\sqrt{169}$

(5) $\sqrt{196}$

(6) $\sqrt{225}$

(7) $\sqrt{256}$

(8) $\sqrt{324}$

(9) $\sqrt{400}$

Finding a square root.

Here is an efficient strategy for finding a square root of any number.

This method is that of trial and improvement.

Start with a number whose square root you want to find
(a calculator or a spreadsheet may be useful for the later part of this example)

Step1: Guess a number

Step2: Divide this number into the number whose square root you want

Step3: Take the average of the this answer and the initial guess

Repeat steps 2 and 3 until you get a very good approximation

Example 1: Find $\sqrt{12}$.

Step 1: Let us say we guess 3 as the answer.

Step 2: Divide 12 by 3 to get 4

Step 3: Take average of the two numbers (3+4)/2 =3.5

We know that 35 X 35 =1225 so 3.5 X 3.5 = 12.25. Let us see if we can improve our answer.

Now divide 12 by 3.5 =$12 \div 3\frac{1}{2}$ =$12 \div \frac{7}{2}$ =12 X 2/7 =24/7 =3and 3/7

Now, $3\frac{3}{7}$ =3.43 approximately.

Take the average of 3.5+3.43 which gives (3.5+3.43)/2=3.465

.

Now square 3.465, we find that 3.465 X 3.465=12.006225, which is very near 12!

So 3.465 is a good answer for $\sqrt{12}$. See if you get an even a better answer. You may use a calculator or a spreadsheet!

If you begin with a good guess to start with you can get a very good approximation in two trials.

Cubes and Cube Roots

A cube of number is written as x^3.

So for example 5^3 means 5X5X5 =125

Similarly,

6^3 =6 X 6 X 6 = 216

7^3 =7 X 7 X 7 = 343

8^3 =8 X 8 X 8 = 512

9^3 = 9 X 9 X 9 = 729

10^3 = 10 X 10 X 10 = 1000

Cube Roots

Cube roots are found by finding a number which when cubed gives you the number inside the cube root.

So for example the cube root of 125 is written as $\sqrt[3]{125}$

Also we know that 5X5X5 =125, so that $\sqrt[3]{125}$ =5

Finding cube roots of perfect cubes.

Look at the last digit of the cubes of the first 9 numbers.

1^3	2^3	3^3	4^3	5^3	6^3	7^3	8^3	9^3
1	8	27	64	125	216	343	512	729

You can see from the above that the cube roots of numbers ending in 1, 4, 6 and 9 also end in the same respective numbers.

Also, the cube root of numbers ending in 2, 3, 5, 7 and 8 will end in the difference from 10 in the last figure. This means the cube root of numbers ending in 2, 3, 5, 7 and 8 will end in 8, 7, 5, 3 and 2.

Hence, we can predict the last digit of a cube root by looking at the last digit of the cube.

Example 1: Find the cube root of 1728

We know that 10x10X10 =1000

And 20X20X20 is 8000

So the answer should be much nearer 10. Now since the last digit of the cube is 8, this means the last digit of the cube root is 2.

So the cube root of 1728 is 12

Example 2: Find the cube root of 12,167

Again we know that 10X10X10 =1000

And 20X20X20 =8000

It seems the answer is over 20.

Since the last digit of the cube is 7, this means the last digit of the cubic root is 3.

So the cube root of 12,167 is 23

Chapter 19

Introduction to Algebra

The word 'algebra' comes from the Arabic al-jebr, which means 'the reuniting of broken parts'. By implication this means the equating of like to like.

In algebra we often use letters instead of numbers. There are some basic conventions and rules of algebra that you should be familiar with to progress in this subject. This chapter will be useful from 10 years of age onwards. However, some kids at 9 might benefit too.

If you see	We mean
$x = y$	x equals y
$x > y$	x is greater than y
$x < y$	x is less than y
$x \geq y$	x is greater than or equal to y
$x \leq y$	x is less than or equal to y
$x + y$	the sum of x and y
$x - y$	subtract y from x
xy	x times y
x/y	x divided by y
$x \div y$	x divided by y
x^n	x to the power n
$x(x + y)$	x times the sum of $x + y$

Also note that:

$x(x + y) = x^2 + xy$

$x^2 (x + x^2 + y) = x^3 + x^4 + x^2 y$

In general, a x a x a x a ....(n times) $= a^n$

You also need to know these algebraic rules for the multiplication and division of positive and negative numbers.

Multiplying positive and negative numbers.

(+) X (+) = + (a plus number times a plus number gives us a plus number)

(+) X (−) = − (a plus number times a minus number gives us a minus number)

(−) X (+) = − (a minus number times a plus number gives us a minus number)

(−) X (−) = + (a minus number times a minus number gives us a plus number)

Dividing positive and negative numbers.

(+) ÷ (+) = + (a plus number divided by a plus number gives us a plus number)

(+) ÷ (−) = − (a plus number divided by a minus number gives us a minus number)

(−) ÷ (+) = − (a minus number divided by a plus number gives us a minus number)

(−) ÷ (−) = + (a minus number times a minus number gives us a plus number)

Summary: <u>For both multiplication and division, like signs gives us a plus sign and unlike signs gives a minus sign</u>

Also when adding and subtracting it is worth knowing that:

When you add two minus numbers you get a bigger minus number.

Example 1: −4 − 6 = −10

When you add a plus number and a minus number you get the sign corresponding to the bigger number as shown below:

Example 2: +6 − 9 = −3, whereas, −6 + 9 = 3

When you subtract a minus from a plus or minus number you need to note the results as shown below:

Example 3: 6 −(− 3) we get 6+3 =9 (since −(−3) =+3)

Example 4: 7 −(+3) we get 7 − 3 =4 (since −(+3) =−3)

In this case note that − (−) =+. Also, +(−) =− and −(+) =−.

Finally you need to know the rules concerning the operation of numbers:

By operations we mean working out powers of numbers, multiplication, division, addition and subtraction. These operations need to be performed in the right order. Failing to do this might give you wrong results.

The rule taught traditionally is that of **BIDMAS**.

The **BIDMAS** rule is as follows:

(1) Always work out the **B**racket(s) first

(2) Then work out the **I**ndices of a number (squares, cubes, square roots and so on)

(3) Now **M**ultiply and **D**ivide

(4) Finally do the **A**ddition and **S**ubtraction.

Example 1: Work out 2(4+6) − 4

Work out the bracket first then times by 2 to get 2 X 10 =20. Finally take away 4 to get 16

So 2(4+6) − 4 =16

Example 2: $3 \times 4^2 + 13(7 - 2)$

The first part is 3 X 16 (we square before multiplying)

The second part is 13 X 5 (we do the brackets and then multiply)

The first part is thus 48 and the second part 65. Adding these two parts together we have 113.

So, $3 \times 4^2 + 13(7 - 2) = 113$

Simplifying algebraic expressions.

Example 1: Simplify 3x +4x +5x

Method: We simple add up all the x's.

Hence we get 3x+4x+5x = 12x

Example2: Simplify 3x +4x +3y +5y
Method: Add up all the like terms.
So we get 3x+4x +3y+5y = 7x +8y
(Notice we add up all the x's and all the y's)

Example 3: Simplify 3m +4y +2m −3y
Method: as before, we add and subtract like terms.
Now 3m+2m =5m and 4y-3y =1y or just y.
So we can write 3m +4y +2m −3y = 5m + y.

Example 4: Simplify 3m +3n −2(2m+4n)
Method: Using the rules we learnt earlier, we have:
3m +3n −2(2m+4n)= 3m +3n −4m − 8n
Notice that we get −4m −8n since −2x2m =−4m and −2x4n = −8n
Finally 3m +3n −4m −8n = −m −5n

Now try these yourself.

Ex19A:

Simplify the following expressions:
- (1)   3x + 6x
- (2)   4n - 2n
- (3)   4x +3x +6m +3m
- (4)   6t +5t +7k − 3k
- (5)   6m +7m + 3n +7n −2n
- (6)   6y +5r +6t +4r +3r
- (7)   7t +8m +9t +6m
- (8)   8y+7y +8t −3y −2t

Multiplying out brackets.
Example 1: Expand 3(2x +5)

Method: we multiply 3 by each term in the bracket. So we get 3 X 2x +3 X 5 which gives us 6x + 15.

Example 2: Expand and simplify 3(2x +5) +4(2x+7)

Method: Multiply 3 by each term in the first bracket then 4 by each term in the second bracket. The final step is to simplify by collecting up the like terms.

3(2x+5) +4(2x+7) =6x+15+8x+28 =14x + 43

Notice the last step is simply adding 6x + 8x and then 15+28.

Example 3: Work out 5(2x -5) – 6(3x – 4)

This gives us 10x–25 –18x +24 = –8x –1

Example 4: Work out (2x+3)(2x+4)

When we have to multiply out two brackets we have to multiply each term in the first bracket by each term in the second bracket. We then simplify the resulting expression as before. An easy way to multiply out two brackets is to use the grid method as shown below:

First put each of the terms of each bracket on the outside grid as shown

X	2x	+3
2x		
+4		

Step2: Multiply each outside term together. So that for example 2x X 2x =$4x^2$. The other results are shown inside the grid.

X	2x	+ 3
2x	$4x^2$	+ 6x
+ 4	8x	+12

After multiplying out the terms, the answer is found by adding all the terms inside the grid and simplifying the resulting expression.

So we have, $4x^2$ + 6x + 8x +12 (These are all the terms inside the grid)

Finally, $4x^2 + 6x + 8x + 12 = 4x^2 + 14x + 12$

Another example will help consolidate the process:
Multiply out $(2x - 3)(3x + 2)$

Put the terms of each bracket on the outside of the grid as shown

X	2x	−3
3x	$6x^2$	− 9x
+ 2	4x	− 6

Collecting up all the terms inside the grid we have:

$6x^2 - 9x + 4x - 6$

Now simplify which gives us, $6x^2 - 5x - 6$

Chapter 20

Algebraic Substitution.

This is the process of substituting numbers for letters and working out value of the corresponding expression.

Example 1: if a =5 and b=6 work out 2a +3b

Method: Substitute numbers for letters and we get:

2 X 5+3 X 6

(Notice 2a means 2 X a and 3b means 3 X b)

So, 2 X 5 +3 X 6 = 10+18 =28

This means that 2a+3b =28

Example 2: If m=7 and n=8 work out 5m– 3n

Substituting numbers for letters we get:

5 X 7 – 3 X 8 = 35 – 24= 11

So 5m –3n =11

Example 3: If k=6 and t=8 work out 2(4k–2t) +kt

Substituting the values of k and t we have:

2(4 X 6–2 X 8) + 6 X 8

=2 X (24-16) +48 = 2 X 8 +48 =16+48 =64

So 2(4k-2t) +kt = 64

Example 4: If t=9 and u= 6 work out $3t^2$ -5u

Substituting appropriately we get:

3×9^2 - 5 X 6 = 3 X 81–30 =243-30 =213

(Notice, we use the BIDMAS rule to work out the square first and then do the multiplication)

So, $3t^2$ -5u =213

Now try these.

Ex20A:

(1) If a=7 and b=11 work out 3a+5b

(2) If m=8 and n=3 work out 5m − 4n

(3) If x=12 and y =4 work out 3(3x −4y) + 2xy

(4) If s=8 and t= 9 work out $3s^2$ +5(2t − s)

(5) If p=13 and q =14 work out 12p +q/2 − 11q

(6) If x= −4 and y =8 work out 2x − 3y

(7) If b= −6 and c= −9 work out $3b^2$ +2c

(8) If t=9 and u = -7 work out 4t +5u

Chapter 21

Simple Equations

Consider the following English statements and their mathematical equivalent:

English Statements	Algebra
Something plus five equals ten	$x + 5 = 10$
Something times two, plus five equals eleven	$2x + 5 = 11$
Something times three, minus five equals thirteen	$3x - 5 = 13$
Something divided by two equals three	$x/2 = 3$

Now consider solving these equations using a common sense approach.

Example 1: Something plus five equals ten. What is 'something'?

Clearly we need to add five to five to get ten. So 'something' in this case equals five.

Solving this by algebra can be very similar. As we saw, we can re-write the English statement above in algebra as follows:

$x + 5 = 10$ (notice, we are representing 'something' by x)

Now, if $x + 5 = 10$ clearly x (which represents 'something') is equal to 5.

So, $x = 5$

Example 2: 'Something' times two plus five equals eleven. Find the 'something'.

We know that 'something' times two plus five equals eleven.

So the two times 'something' must equal 6. In which case 'something' must be 3.

Now consider the algebraic equivalent.

$2x + 5 = 11$

This means $2x = 6$

Which means $x = 3$

Now consider a more formal method.

Imagine an equation like a balance. Whatever you do to one side you must do to the other.

Example 1: Solve the equation $x + 5 = 10$

Subtract 5 from both sides

So, $x = 5$

However, we can also use the method of taking inverses.

The rules are: When something is added to the x-term subtract, when something is subtracted from the x-term then add. When x, is multiplied, by a number we divide. Finally, when the x-term, is divided, by a number we multiply.

Example 2: Solve the equation $2x + 5 = 11$

Subtract 5 from both sides (that is, take the inverse of +5)

So, $2x = 6$

Now divide both sides by 2 (that is, take the inverse of X2)

So, $x = 3$.

Example 3: Solve the equation $3x - 5 = 13$

This time add 5 to both sides giving:

$3x = 18$

Now divide both sides by 3 which gives, $x = 6$

Summary:

The key point to remember is that you reverse the operation to eliminate a number from one side. This is called the method of taking inverses. So if $x + 5 = 10$ then to get rid of the 5 from the left hand side we subtract 5 from both sides. Similarly if, $3x = 18$ then divide both sides by 3 to find x.

Now try these.

Ex21A:

Solve the following equations:

(1) $x + 5 = 16$

(2) $x - 5 = 13$

(3) $x - 13 = 24$

(4) $2x + 3 = 13$

(5) $2x - 5 = 15$

(6) $3x - 12 = 18$

(7) $4x + 5 = 45$

(8) $9x - 6 = 93$

(9) $11x - 121 = 11$

Now consider slightly harder equations:

Example 1: Solve the equation $5x - 1 = 2x + 8$

First add 1 to both sides, which gives:

$5x = 2x + 9$

Now subtract 2x from both sides to give $3x = 9$

Finally divide both sides by 3 to get x=3.

(Notice each step simplifies the equation further)

Example 2: Solve the equation $5(2x + 1) = 4(2x + 1)$

To solve this first multiply out the bracket which gives:

$10x + 5 = 8x + 4$

(Multiply each term outside the bracket by each term inside the bracket)

Now subtract 5 from both sides, which gives:

$10x = 8x - 1$

Now subtract 8x from both sides, which gives:

2x = –1

Finally, divide both sides by 2 to get x= –1/2 or –0.5

Example 3: Solve the equation $\dfrac{2x}{3} + 5 = 7$

We can simplify this to $\dfrac{2x}{3} = 2$ (by subtracting 5 from both sides)

Now multiply both sides by 3 to get the expression below:

2x =6

So x =3

Example 4: Solve the inequality 2x +5>9

This simply says 2x + 5 is greater than 9. To find x still use the rules of a simple equation. That is, whatever you do to one side you must do to the other.

If 2x +5>9

Then 2x >4 (by taking away 5 from both sides)

Now, divide both sides by 2 to get x >2. Our answer for x is all values greater than 2.

Now try solving these equations.

Ex21B:

(1) 2x + 1 =x +5

(2) 3x +2 = 2x +8

(3) 3x +7 =5x – 8

(4) 3(3x – 1) =2(2x +1)

(5) 7(2x – 1) =5(2x +1)

(6) 3(2x – 1) = 6(2x +1) + 3(2x +10)

(7) 8(12x– 12) = 7(12x +6) – 2(3x – 5)

(8) $\dfrac{x}{5} + 7 = 9$

(9) $\dfrac{3x}{4} - 8 = 11$

(10) $\dfrac{6x}{7} - 8 = \dfrac{3x}{4} + 9$

(11) 3x +7 > 8

(12) 4x −11 < 13

(13) 3x +6 > 2x +4

More algebra for solving simple equations:

For those who have managed so far, consider the equation $ax + b = cx + d$

Clearly if we bring all the x terms to the left hand side and the other terms to the right hand side we get: $ax - cx = d - b$

This can be factorised (common term x taken out) into: $x(a - c) = d - b$

Dividing both sides by $a - c$ we get $x = (d - b)/(a - c)$

So to solve any equation such as $13x + 5 = 2x + 3$

We can use the fact that $x = (d - b)/(a - c)$

Which gives $x = (3 - 5)/(13 - 2) = -2/11$ straight away.

Miscellaneous

Even Numbers: All numbers that have 2 as a factor are even numbers.

Examples are: 2, 4, 6, 8, 10, 12, 14, 16

So, 168 is an even number as it can be divided exactly by 2.

Odd Numbers: Are all numbers that do not have 2 as a factor.

Examples: 1, 3, 5, 7, 9, 11, 13, 15, 17

So for example 81 is an odd number, as 2 is not a factor of 81.

Notice something interesting about odd numbers. The cumulative sum of consecutive odd numbers generates square numbers.

The first number is $1 = 1 \times 1 = 1^2$

The sum of the first two numbers is $1 + 3 = 4 = 2 \times 2 = 2^2$

The sum of the first three numbers is $1 + 3 + 5 = 9 = 3 \times 3 = 3^2$

The sum of the first four numbers is $1 + 3 + 5 + 7 = 16 = 4 \times 4 = 4^2$ and so on.

Multiples: These are simply the result of multiplying a given number by integers (whole numbers) so for example the multiples of 8 are 8, 16, 24, 32, 40, 48........

Factors: A factor is a number that divides exactly into another number as for example, the number 2 in the case of even numbers.

3 is a factor of 9, as 3 goes exactly into 9.

15, has two factors other than 15 and 1. The two factors are 5 and 3, since both these numbers go exactly into 15.

Factors of 20 are 1, 2, 4, 5, 10 and 20 (since all these numbers divide exactly into 20)

Prime Numbers: A prime number is a number that has two factors, the number itself and 1. Examples of prime numbers include 2, 3, 5, 7, 11, 13, and 17. So for example 23 is a prime number since it has no other factor besides itself and 1.

Divisibilty by 9:

A number is divisible by 9 if its reduced digit sum is 9.

Example: the number 18 can be reduced to $1+8 = 9$, so 18 is divisible by 9

567 can be reduced to $5 + 6 + 7 = 18$ and $18 = 1 + 8 = 9$. So, 567 is divisible by 9.

59049 can be reduced to $5 + 9 + 0 + 4 + 9 = 27$ and $27 = = 2 + 7 = 9$

Hence, the number, 59049 can be divided by 9.

Value of Π (pi), circumference and area of a circle

This is a useful for children to remember when they are 10 or 11 years old

Remember (π) Pi to 6 decimal places

Π is a useful number for working out the circumference and area of a circle. The value of Π is approximately 3.14 to 2 decimal places, but some children might find it fun to remember it to 6 decimal places!

This is a well-known memory trick to remember Pi to 6 decimal places.
'How I wish I could calculate pi'

You will notice that if you can remember this sentence than Pi can easily be remembered to 6 decimal places.

Simply substitute the number of letters for each word.
How = 3
I = 1
Wish = 4
I =1
Could = 5
Calculate = 9
Pi = 2

This means the value of pi to 6 decimal places is **3.141592**
Make sure you remember the sentence **'How I wish I could calculate Pi'**
You can extend this phrase into a rhyme to remember pi to 18 decimal places

Useful formula for children eager to learn:

Circumference of a circle $= 2\pi r$ (where r is the radius of the circle)

Since, diameter (d) $= 2 \times$ radius we can re-write, circumference $= \pi d$

Area of a circle $= \pi r^2$ (π times radius squared)

Note the value of π is approximately 3.14 (to two decimal places) which is adequate for most calculations.

Useful Formulae

(1) Area of a rectangle = length X width = l X w

(2) Perimeter of rectangle = twice length + twice width = 2l + 2w

(3) Area of a triangle = (base X perpendicular height)/2 = $\dfrac{b \times h}{2}$

Example: Find area of a triangle whose base is 10cm and the perpendicular height is 8cm.

Area of triangle = $\dfrac{b \times h}{2}$ = (10X8)/2 = 40 cm^2

(4) Circumference of a circle = 2πr (where r is the radius of the circle)

Since, diameter (d) = 2x radius we can re-write, circumference = πd

(5) Area of a circle = πr^2 (π times radius squared)

Note the value of π is approximately 3.14 (to two decimal places)

Example: Find area of circle whose radius is 10cm

Area of a circle = πr^2 = 3.14 X 10 X 10 = 3.14 X 100 = 314 cm^2

(6) Volume of a cuboid = length X width X height = l X w X h

(7) To convert temperature readings from Celsius to Fahrenheit use the formula below:

F = $\dfrac{9}{5}$C + 32

Example: If the temperature is 10 degrees Celsius then the equivalent in Fahrenheit is: $\dfrac{9}{5}$ X 10 + 32 = $\dfrac{90}{5}$ + 32 = 18 + 32 = 50

Hence, 10 degrees centigrade = 50 degrees Fahrenheit

(9) To convert Fahrenheit to Celsius use the formula below:

C = 5(F-32)/9

Example: Convert 68 degrees Fahrenheit to degrees Celsius.

C = 5(68 - 32)/9 = 5 X 36/9 = 5 X 4 = 20

Hence, 68 degrees Fahrenheit = 20 degrees Celsius

Common Metric and Imperial Measures

Metric Measurements

1000 millilitres(ml) =1 litre(l)

100 centilitres(cl) =1 litre (l)

10ml =1 cl

1 centimetre(cm) =10 millimetres(mm)

1 metre(m) = 100 cm

1 kilometre (km) =1000 m

1 kilogram (kg) =1000 grams (g)

Imperial Measurements

1 foot =12 inches

1 yard =3 feet

1 pound = 16 ounces

1 stone =14 pounds (lb)

1 gallon = 8 pints

Useful conversions from one to the other

1 km = 5/8 mile

1 mile =8/5 km

1kg =2.2 lb (approximately)

1 gallon =4.5 litres (approximately)

1 inch = 2.54 cm (approximately)

Answers to questions set

Chapter1	Chapter2	Chapter2
Ex1A	Ex2A	Ex2B
(1) 25	(1) 3	(1) 194
(2) 31	(2) 4	(2) 196
(3) 44	(3) 13	(3) 2006
(4) 185	(4) 9	(4) 203
(5) 106	(5) 4	(5) 459
(6) 205	(6) 8	(6) 405
(7) 385	(7) 15	(7) 628
(8) 968	(8) 17	(8) 131
	(9) 25	
	(10) 19	

Chapter2	Chapter 3	Chapter3
Ex 2C	Ex3A:	Ex 3B
(1) 343	(1) 56	(1) 182
(2) 33	(2) 72	(2) 195
(3) 493	(3) 63	(3) 192
(4) 1011	(4) 64	(4) 156
(5) 2	(5) 63	(5) 210
(6) 36	(6) 81	(6) 272
(7) 102	(7) 35	(7) 270
(8) 9214	(8) 40	
(9) 979		

Chapter 4	Chapter 5	Chapter 5
Ex4A :	**Ex 5A**	**Ex 5C**
(1) 45600	(1) 253	(1) 72
(2) 548	(2) 451	(2) 96
(3) 78870	(3) 495	(3) 156
(4) 67800	(4) 616	(4) 192
(5) 6.7	(5) 374	(5) 216
(6) 6.87	(6) 363	(6) 264
(7) 0.765		
(8) 8.97	**Ex 5B**	**Ex 5D**
(9) 0.8712	(1) 63	(1) 30
(10) 0.067	(2) 81	(2) 15
	(3) 108	(3) 25
	(4) 126	(4) 35
	(5) 153	(5) 10
	(6) 198	(6) 40
	(7) 189	(7) 45
	(8) 216	

Chapter 7	Chapter 8	Chapter 9
Ex7A	**Ex 8A**	**Ex9A**
(1) 9120	(1) 196	(1) 1225
(2) 8096	(2) 225	(2) 2025
(3) 7176	(3) 256	(3) 3025
(4) 11016	(4) 289	(4) 5625
(5) 11024	(5) 324	(5) 72.25
(6) 8075	(6) 361	(6) 902.5
(7) 8091		(7) 11025
(8) 9025		(8) 38025
(9) 13216		

Chapter 9	Chapter 11	Chapter 12
Ex9B	Ex11A	Ex12A
(1) 9021	(1) $275	(1) 22, 27
(2) 7216	(2) $125	(2) 49, 64
(3) 4221	(3) $240	(3) 1331, 14641
(4) 2016	(4) $45	(4) 8, 13
(5) 7221	(5) $900	(5) 6.25, 3.125
(6) 9016	(6) $150	(6) −2, −7
(7) 15616	(7) $100	(7) 625, 3125
(8) 15621	(8) $675	(8) 1, ¼
(9) 13216	(9) $5,600	(9) 729, 6561
(10) 24016	(10) $2392.74	
(11) 27221	(11) $5864.29	
(12) 38024	(12) $3,600	
(13) 164016	(13) £20	

Chapter 12	Chapter 13	Chapter 13
Ex 12B	Ex13A	Ex13A
(1) 26, 31	(1)	(2)
(2) 100, 121	(a) 430	(a) 4600
(3) 2662, 2982	(b) 560	(b) 6500
	(c) 4680	(c) 600
(4) 23, 29	(d) 50	(d) 200
(5) .5, 3.75	(e) 6750	(e) 2300
(6) 256, 1024	(f) 6670	(f) 6600
(7) 25, 6.25		
(8) 343, 2401		

Chapter 13	**Chapter 13**	**Chapter 15**
Ex13A(3)	**Ex13A(4)**	**Ex15A**
(a) 56000	(a) 45.3	(1) 23643
(b) 56000	(b) 12.5	(2) 71806
(c) 64000	(c) 1.1	(3) 54384
(d) 65000	(d) 123.6	(4) 145092
(e) 11000		(5) 318331
(f) 123000	**Ex13A (5)**	(6) 722502
	(a) 1	(7) 13018
	(b) 4	(8) 58725
	(c) 1	(9) 312221
	(d) 0	(10) 9225

Chapter16
Ex16A

(1) 13/20
(2) 23/56
(3) $1\frac{1}{6}$
(4) $\frac{26}{35}$
(5) 17/36
(6) 11/21
(7) 25/26
(8) 27/132
(9) $-1\frac{4}{65}$
(10) 1/176

Chapter16
Ex16B

(1) $6\frac{23}{40}$
(2) $10\frac{16}{21}$
(3) $5\frac{49}{99}$
(4) $3\frac{13}{35}$
(5) $5\frac{15}{143}$

Chapter16
Ex16C

(1) $3\frac{9}{14}$
(2) $5\frac{5}{8}$
(3) 7
(4) $1\frac{5}{6}$
(5) 3
(6) 2

Chapter17
Ex17A

(1) (a) John = $200
    (b) Ben = $300
(2) 80 kg
(3) 3m

Chapter18
Ex18A

(1) 9
(2) 12
(3) 8
(4) 13
(5) 14
(6) 15
(7) 16
(8) 18
(9) 20

Chapter19
Ex19A

(1) 9x
(2) 2n
(3) 7x + 9m
(4) 11t + 4k
(5) 13m + 8n
(6) 6(y + 2r + t)
(7) 2(8t + 7m)
(8) 6(2y − t)

Chapter20	Chapter21	Chapter21
Ex20A	Ex21A	Ex21B
(1) 76	(1) $x=11$	(1) $x=4$
(2) 28	(2) $x=18$	(2) $x=6$
(3) 156	(3) $x=37$	(3) $x=7.5$
(4) 242	(4) $x=5$	(4) $x=1$
(5) 9	(5) $x=10$	(5) $x=3$
(6) −32	(6) $x=10$	(6) $x=-3.25$
(7) 90	(7) $x=10$	(7) $x=8\frac{2}{9}$
(8) 1	(8) $x=11$	(8) $x=10$
	(9) $x=12$	(9) $x=25\frac{1}{3}$
		(10) $x=158\frac{2}{3}$
		(11) $x>\frac{1}{3}$
		(12) $x<6$
		(13) $x>-2$

Printed in Poland
by Amazon Fulfillment
Poland Sp. z o.o., Wrocław